In My Father's House Again

Valinda Johnson

Order this book online at **www.trafford.com**
or email orders@trafford.com

Most Trafford titles are also available at major online book retailers.

Front cover and author photo by Sandy McCurdy.
Back cover photo by Terry Holub, Fontanelle Observer.

Printed in the United States of America.

ISBN: 978-1-4269-7506-6 (sc)
ISBN: 978-1-4269-7507-3 (e)

Trafford rev. 07/21/2011

 www.trafford.com

North America & International
toll-free: 1 888 232 4444 (USA & Canada)
phone: 250 383 6864 ♦ fax: 812 355 4082

Special Recognition

I want to thank all of my friends, family and classmates who not only made growing up in a small town so special but also helped with suggestions, memories and offered encouragement.

This story is as true as I could make it. Any discrepancies are due entirely to my memory not being completely accurate.

In My Father's House Again

In Memory of My Mother

Introduction

Returning to Iowa after 45 years to help Dad became a challenge as well as a pleasant adventure. I had not anticipated Dad would be moody and demanding. I heard many stories about the problems others my age had in dealing with their parents' aging problems but I was sure my Dad would not be so difficult. Dad was much too active physically and mentally for a nursing home, too independent for assisted living and an apartment was out of the question. What would he do with all he had accumulated in 94 years?

I took over household chores like washing, cleaning, and cooking. Robert was looking forward to taking over the numerous tasks of maintaining the buildings and grounds making it possible for Dad to stay in his home as long as we were able to care for him. My husband's retirement was nine months away and he could then join my granddaughter and me.

Dad's best friend and classmate had a hard time with her children. They did not think it was safe for her to continue living by herself. She was moved to an apartment against her wishes and then the children thought it also necessary to take control of her finances. As his friend went through her difficulties, he feared I would do the same things to him.

My Southern-born and raised husband loved Iowa. After visiting in Iowa a few times he told me he wanted to live there when he retired. I was not so eager to return and told him he could go if he wanted—without me. It took years to be comfortable with who I was. My husband and friends did not realize the emotional conflicts I suffered or contributions they made to help me understand the past was unimportant and that it was okay to be myself. Before I could face the challenges of helping Dad, I had to deal with the ghosts of my past and resolve those issues.

CHAPTER ONE

"Deb, are you ready to go?" I asked. We were about to start on a journey that would change everything in our lives. Deb picked up her huge bag of sunflower seeds, gave poppa a hug and a kiss, told Dexter, our long-haired Dachshund, goodbye and headed for the SUV.

"We are going to miss you so much," I told my husband, Robert or Poppa as Deb calls him, and miss him we would. He had us both spoiled.

"Be careful," he told me as he closed the car door. "Don't drive if you get sleepy."

"I won't," I promised. We both knew all too well how hard it was on some occasions for me to stay awake on the road. "Deb will help me. Won't you, baby?" She nodded. She had first-hand knowledge of a dozing and driving episode when we returned from our last trip to Iowa.

It was about a year ago I was called to Iowa for an emergency visit with Dad.

"Valinda, I think you might want to come and check on your Dad." It was a call from my sister-in-law, Marsha. Marsha always called me when things were serious because she thought I could do more with Dad than anyone else could.

I was at work when she called. "What is going on?"

"We aren't exactly sure," she continued. "He had a fall down a flight of stairs the other night when he was at a dance at Williamson. He was going to the bathroom and he went to the wrong door. Instead of opening the bathroom door he opened the door to the basement. When he stepped inside to turn the light on his foot unexpectedly landed on the first step downward. He lost his balance but managed to grab a hand rail as he slid down the stairs. He seemed to be okay afterward. He danced and drove himself home. But now he won't leave the thermostat alone. I have been with him most of today. Irene is coming to stay with him in the morning." Irene has been Dad's girlfriend for over 20 years.

The fall was reason for plenty of concern even though he was all right but it played on my mind the rest of the day wondering why the thermostat issue was significant enough to mention. Surely there was more to this than I knew. After work I called Irene. "What is going on with Dad?"

"Oh, I don't know. Maybe he had a stroke." I heard the apprehensive tone in her voice. "He's been talking to people who aren't there. Marsha swept the floor and then he told her some lady was sweeping it again and she had a little girl with her. Then he saw people on the front porch and a group in the living room. I'll be with him in the morning and will stay until you can get here," Irene assured me.

Whoa, now that got my attention. Three more weeks and I would be retired but this could not wait. "I will be there in two days," I said.

I packed that night and left the following morning. Driving alone and staying awake was not much of a problem on that trip. I could tune the radio to a peppy country music station and sing along since no one would be listening. As long as the cruise control was set, I would not drive to the beat of the music. Seven hundred miles was a two-day drive for me so I spent the night in Sedalia, Missouri. After settling into the motel room with the remote in hand, I received another call. It was Irene. "Your Dad fell again," she told me. "He fell on the porch steps and skinned his arm pretty badly. He won't go to the doctor." His injury from the fall on the two front steps was much worse than he had incurred on an entire flight of stairs at the dance.

When I arrived Irene quickly packed her bag and was ready to leave for her home. Dad was extremely difficult to deal with and she didn't want to stay any longer. "By the way, Valinda," she began, "your dad has made some people pretty unhappy. The lumber yard won't sell him overalls anymore and the heat and air company won't take his calls."

I called to make an appointment with his doctor to check his badly scraped arm but Dr. Pearce was not available and I had to schedule his appointment with another doctor. Dad threw a fit. "Gawd damn it. I am not going to that doctor," he stormed. If I thought I could be his caretaker, as Marsha and Irene hoped, we were all in for some unpleasant surprises.

"All right, all right, calm down." I raised my hands hoping to block the angry barrage of words. I cancelled the appointment and waited until he could see his usual doctor.

He continued to be obsessed with the thermostat. He sat on the arm of the couch and watched it with a flashlight in hand even in daylight. If it varied one degree from its setting Dad was upset. It was spring but the temperatures were still cool and I never knew if he would have it set to air conditioning or heat. After managing his household for over sixty years he should not have problems understanding the temperature controls but he did. I tried to explain to him how it worked but it was useless. I finally reached the end of my patience and asked, "If you are wrong about something, do you want to know?" It was a trick question that I didn't expect to get a straight answer to. He was good at giving indirect answers to avoid being cornered but this time he took the bait.

Hesitantly he spoke, "Yes, I want to know."

"You are wrong. Please leave the thermostat alone," I stated emphatically fully expecting another outrage to ensue but it didn't. He just dropped his eyes and remained silent.

Maybe this was the time to ask him about the invisible people he talked to. "Did you have some visitors recently," I asked.

"There were a bunch of them in the living room," he admitted. "They didn't talk to me so I took a yardstick in there and poked them in the bellies. They didn't move so I knew they weren't really there. I just went on to bed." He was seeing things but he wasn't stupid.

After a few doctor visits for his arm and sinus infections and getting him to understand that he had to finish all of his antibiotics exactly as directed, he finally returned to his usual self. The only explanation the doctor could come up with regarding his mental state was that the swelling in his sinuses may have put some pressure on his brain.

By this time it was too late for me to return to Arkansas for my retirement party. Since Deb was out of school and she and Robert would arrive in a few days for our usual July vacation, I decided to wait for them even though it meant we would have both vehicles in Iowa.

CHAPTER TWO

After Robert and Deb's arrival we settled into our usual routine. We relaxed and enjoyed the Independence Day celebration which was as pleasant as ever. Watching the parade from the front yard of my Dad's house was a treat – entertainment without going anywhere. It was a short parade compared to the Sesquicentennial parade three years ago.

This 12 square block town of around 600 people, a large number of whom are retired, was amazing in that it could drum up so much participation. The Sesquicentennial parade was awesome. It lasted for two hours and was so long that the end of the parade and the beginning could have overlapped several blocks. The parade committee's original goal was to have one horse for each of the hundred and fifty years since the town was founded. I don't think they missed it by very much.

Even though things are different now, this was a wonderful opportunity for Deb to experience a little of what I enjoyed as a child. The carnival no longer comes to town but community ingenuity created lots of entertainment.

Miniature golf, donkey rides, bossy bingo, bed races, mud volleyball, Doofus Doolittle a comedian and fiddler from Branson, Missouri, a ventriloquist, stories of the Underground Railroad were told in the library, pony rides, miniature train rides with the engine being a well-disguised riding lawn mower, horse-drawn wagon rides, buggy rides and a number of other home-spun games were enough to amuse all ages.

A huge tent was set up on the street for the Alumni Banquet meal and entertainment that included a most entertaining three-legged man routine. Karen, my childhood friend, was a part of the committee that organized and coordinated the activities. We had never had a three-day celebration before and this one was a rip-roaring success.

Not only was the Alumni Banquet scheduled for the Fourth but there were family reunions and a 50th class reunion for the class of 1965. Each event drew a different crowd. The park and streets were full of people every day. The 4-H groups cooked and served breakfast each morning; there was a hot meal for lunch, pancake supper on one night and what we called a "slab" supper on another.

Annual slab suppers became customary in the late 50's when an outdoor roller skating rink was built.

It became the center of activity. It was also where I discovered growing up might be fun.

Wednesday and Saturday nights were skate nights. Everyone in the family cleaned up and dressed up. Moms and dads went up town to watch the kids skate, or snack at the local cafés, or buy groceries. My Mom and Dad said they liked to sit in the car and watch people. Sometimes Dad would buy a bag of fresh roasted peanuts from Frankie Rice's peanut stand. I was at the skating rink going around in circles until it closed at 10:00.

It is funny how our minds select specific incidents to remember. Some are good, some are bad and some are embarrassing. I remember my first bra and the first time I wore it skating. Mom decided it was time that I start wearing it so I put it on. It was too big but it was padded. I checked to make sure the bra would hold its shape. I didn't want to get caught with one side dented in. I put on a dress with elastic waist and elastic neckline. To my surprise, one of the boys asked me to skate the couples' skate. Not only was it the first time a guy had asked me to skate, he was older. He put his right hand on my waist at the back and my left arm stretched across his chest so my hand rested in his hand. Then I realized it. He noticed the difference. I was a little embarrassed. Surely he knew that it wasn't all me inside that dress. Oh well. I didn't care. I was having fun. I had crossed over from being just a little kid to a girl. The kind of girl that guys notice!

The slab is not nearly so popular now. The slab suppers aren't even held there anymore. The new fire station moves the fire trucks outside and hosts them.

This 4th of July was much quieter but still pleasant. We walked the two blocks to the town square several times during the day. Each visit presented something different to do. We always had to eat one of Wayne's famous corndogs and cool off with a snow cone, check out the beer garden and sit on the bleachers in front of the bandstand to watch entertainment and at night, the fireworks display at the football field was as fine as any.

The rest of Robert's vacation was spent helping Dad with the routine upkeep of the property. Dad was prone to doing things a man his age just should not do. A few years ago he had a new metal roof put on the house and more than once I saw him climbing the twenty-foot ladder to check on the quality of work being done. Scolding him did not have any effect on his behavior. Independent as he was, he was glad to have Robert's help and began to make mental notes of things he needed help doing. Every night after supper Dad would ask, "What's up tomorrow?" He could not be idle.

If Robert mentioned a project for the next day Dad would ask, "Want to do it now?"

Robert accomplishes a great deal but paces himself. "No, Ivan. We need something to do tomorrow." "Your Dad could worry the tits off a boar hog," he would always tell me later.

All too soon Robert's vacation was drawing to a close and we had to get everything in order before our return to Arkansas. Dad decided it was time to let us take his camper home with us. It had set unused in the shed for over ten years and there were several things that needed to be updated. After cleaning, replacing tires and battery and a couple other minor fixes, it was hitched to the pickup. Robert and Dexter D. Dachshund (his full registered name) boarded his truck and Deb climbed in the SUV with me. We tested our walkie-talkies to be sure we could stay in communication. Deb and I would be the map readers and leaders. I was a little tense knowing that if I got Robert and the camper off track it might be difficult to find a way to get us all back on the right path but I did well with Deb in control of the map. We made the first day without any major problems until late afternoon.

My eyes began to tire and my lids became heavy. I rolled my window down and searched for peppy music but it was not helping. My tires were often hitting the ribbed shoulder. There was no way I could keep the van evenly directed on the pavement. Desperately I began looking for a place to stop. Then without warning my eyelids dropped and I was asleep for only an instant but it was enough time for the van to dip onto the ribbed shoulder again. It frightened me so that I pulled off the road and stopped. We were safe but I knew how it could have ended and I would not take that chance again. We quickly found a place to park the camper and spent the night.

Now, almost exactly one year later, I was on the road again with Deb, my first grandchild and my only granddaughter. She was born approximately sixteen weeks early, weighing in at only one pound and thirteen ounces. At three months she had finally reached four pounds and thirteen ounces and the hospital called to tell me she was ready to be released. Neither her mother nor father was able to care for her delicate condition. "What should I do?" I asked my precious husband.

"Go get that girl," he told me and I did. The hospital was over 200 miles from my home and required that I stay for two days and nights to be sure not only that I was comfortable caring for her but that they felt she would be safe with me. I saw her tiny little body lying in her bed next to a new born eleven pound baby. She had a frown on her face. "The light is hurting her eyes." I told the nurses. The bright light above her was hard on her premature eyes. The nurse realized I was sensitive to Deb's condition and moved her to an area with less direct lighting.

Deb had not eaten from a bottle until the day I arrived and didn't even know how to suck. We began feeding her every hour. It was difficult to get even an ounce down her each time.

"She's no bigger than a fox squirrel," was Robert's first comment when he laid Deb on his shoulder for the first time. I turned 50 just days before Deb's arrival and was reluctant to start raising another child. It was fun to have a little girl in the house and once she entered our door, we became the parents she needed and we could not imagine being without her.

CHAPTER THREE

Deborah was excited on our trip to Iowa, but she had mixed emotions about leaving behind so many friends and familiar surroundings. We always found ways to make our trips fun. This time Deb created memories by photographing things of interest she found along the way. Sometimes it was a landmark, or a mountain but she also found special interest sites such as a particular road sign, a farm, an artist's painting on the side of a building or the driver of a car next to us. The sunflower seeds were always within her reach. It was warm in late May so she ate and spit hulls out the window all the time we were on the road. I was just glad she was eating them somewhere other than the house where I <u>once</u> found that she had practiced her seed-spitting on the TV screen. She was appropriately scolded even though I knew it was probably one of her "poor judgment" days when she had not taken her ADHD medications.

I made the trip a little more interesting by taking some unplanned side trips. Somewhere along the way while being distracted by one of the frequent calls from Robert, I took highway 169 instead of highway 69. That little trip took us across the Missouri line into Kansas before I realized where we were. Fortunately it was not a long detour.

On the second day we crossed the Missouri line into my home state, Iowa. Deb pulled a few seeds from her bag and tossed them out the window to celebrate. "Wheeee," she sang with glee. There were so many things she knew she had to adjust to, but she was glad to have an interesting summer ahead.

Five miles before we reached our destination we passed through Greenfield. I noticed trees planted on either side of highway 92; their branches touched in the middle making an arch over the road resembling a tunnel. As I left the town the tunnel's arch framed a delightful view of the countryside including an old white barn with a new green metal roof, silos and a farm house.

There was a wonderful fresh quality to the air that felt rejuvenating. Never before had I appreciated the beauty of the rolling hills with patterned fields of corn and soybeans growing.

We were only minutes away from my birthplace where we would find my 94 year-old father waiting. He would be glad to see us but I wondered how he would respond to the changes that our presence would make in his routine. The back of the SUV was packed with everything that could be gotten into it — clothes, shoes, a vacuum cleaner, even a cedar chest. Unpacking and moving those things into the two upstairs bedrooms would be the beginning of a different life for all of us.

CHAPTER FOUR

It had been a difficult decision to make. The hardest part was leaving Robert behind. He decided he would continue working until his 64th birthday. We knew that, because of his health problems, insurance would be high until he turned 65 but we would just have to make the sacrifice. Dad was going to need us more as he aged. He had refused numerous invitations to stay with us or even to visit us. "People here know me and watch out for me," He would say.

Dad was 700 miles from our Arkansas home. Three times in the last year I had to travel to Iowa because of problems he was having and this was the fourth. It seemed more practical to move to Iowa where I could keep a closer eye on him and know exactly what was happening. This time it was his driving that had caused enough concern to make our trip necessary.

A few weeks before we left Arkansas I received word from a friend, who was watching out for him, that he saw Dad's car about two blocks from his home. It appeared he ran into two parked cars. In a town of less than 700 with minimal traffic and wide streets, it should not have happened. When I asked Dad about it his comment was, "They weren't parked where they should have been". My husband and I discussed it and decided the time had come to start making our transition to Iowa. Deborah and I would leave as soon as the school year was over. Robert would retire the following March and then join us. That would give him time to sell the house while I tried to keep Dad off the roads as much as possible. We knew that would be a challenge.

When I arrived, I asked Dad about the accident. You've heard the saying, "That's my story and I'm sticking to it". Dad stuck to his. He said, "I told the officer I was reaching for a phone book on the floor and pulled the steering wheel into the cars before rising back up." I knew the part about "I told the Officer" sounded suspicious but I didn't say anything at that time. After all, I had just gotten there and wasn't ready to start causing trouble.

In many ways Dad did not need a caregiver but there was definitely something that needed to be addressed. Many questioned his driving ability. Often I got reports that Dad was driving all over the street, sometimes onto curbs, or pulling out in front of people. Disturbing as this news was, more serious things were happening. How could it be they were "never his fault" according to him? And it truly seemed they were not his fault. Not once, but twice a car had pulled out of the cemetery and hit his car. One block from home, "someone" ran into him at a high rate of speed. It was the exact place where my brother had an accident about fifty years ago. Another time, "someone" backed into him as he was driving around the square. Even deer considered him a good target and had run into his car on more than one occasion. These reports were over several years, but we were now receiving alerts more frequently.

The most serious mishap was when he made one of his trips to visit his friend who lived about 60 miles away from his home. He knew he was sleepy but only had about 5 miles to go so he kept on driving. Without warning his eyes closed, and he was instantly asleep.

I looked over the site of the accident a few weeks later and saw what a miracle it was that he was not injured. On either side of the road was a steep bank. A very short distance ahead of him was a bridge railing on the paved, but narrow, two-lane country road.

As he heard his tires on the rough shoulder, his eyes opened and he pulled sharply on the steering wheel over-correcting the direction of the car. The car careened across to the other side and, because of the speed he was traveling, did not go down the embankment. He flew into a fence that was probably 20 feet high. The owner of the property raised exotic animals and had the extra-high fence to keep them from escaping. The loose, roughly-constructed fence did not break. It cradled Dad's car as if it were a catcher's mitt, stretching as it slowed the car's speed and gently set it down in a soft, muddy field. One fence post stabbed through the windshield very near Dad's head. Amazingly, Dad opened the car door and walked away from the accident.

For years Irene had told him he needed to wear an angel pin on his hat to keep him safe. When Dad emerged from his car the cap was still on his head and his guardian angel had taken good care of him.

My second consideration in moving was Deborah's schooling. This would be her first year in high school. She would change school buildings and teachers in Arkansas if we stayed there. Instead of putting the move off until something more serious happened and having to make unplanned changes, we would try to make the transition easier for her. She would have the entire summer to get adjusted.

CHAPTER FIVE

I hoped Deborah would enjoy small town life as much as I had. As I was now appreciating the fresh air and beauty of the countryside, my childhood memories were vivid and pleasant. I sat in the yard and looked across to the house where my first childhood friend lived.

Karen and I played together every chance we got. As preschool children we spent hours playing in the sandbox and picking flowers by the railroad bridge but when we got old enough to venture to the city park by ourselves, we ran from merry-go-round to slide to swings. The small town atmosphere was perfect for children in early 50's. It was safe—small enough that everyone knew everyone and everyone's business. There were many retired people who, I am sure, found entertainment in spending a great deal of their time looking out their windows, watching every movement. Sometimes I think they were like the angels that keep an eye on everything that goes on. Now that I am retired, I do that very thing. I see young mothers walking their children in strollers, older adults walking with their spouse or a dog on a leash, I see children who walk to school. Their parents work and the older children oversee the younger ones making sure they are ready for their day ahead. I see the parents with the lawn mowing service involving their children in the business and teaching them the importance of attention to the smallest details. I also understand now how my parents always knew everything I did when I was a kid. Like the time I took the '57 Chevy south of town to see how fast it would go in a quarter mile. Even though the quarter mile goes right past my grandmother's house and my aunt's house I didn't think they would see me and tell on me.

The swings at the park were always my favorite. Fontanelle probably had the highest swing frame in the county. Karen and I sat on the wooden seats, "pumped" our legs forward and backward, forward and backward. Higher and higher we went until we were nearly horizontal to ground. The chain went slack as our bodies hovered in mid-air. A scary, tummy tickling little jerk frightened us for a split second as the chain tightened and the swing began its descent. The refreshing breeze blew in our faces and tousled our hair.

Mary Herr's large yard was between my house and Karen's. It was a great place to play and games were often organized there. "Annie, Annie, Over," rang out the voice of one of the teammates on the other side of the Herr's garage. Karen was on my side. We stood in silence looking intently at the roof and waiting to see if the ball was going to come over for us to catch. "Pig Tail," the voice called out again and we knew the ball had fallen short of its goal. We had to wait for another "Annie, Annie, Over". This time the ball topped the garage and gently started rolling toward me.

"Catch it! Catch it," Karen called out to me. She ran out behind me knowing I was not positioned to get the ball. I backed up correcting my aim and ran into her and we both rolled on the ground. "I almost had it," she scolded me.

Now it was our turn to throw it over. "Annie, Annie, Over," I announced over and over until I finally was able to get the ball over the roof.

The silence again, waiting to see if they caught the ball. They must have caught the ball! Now the person with the ball was coming after us! Which way will they come around?! We had to be ready to run so they wouldn't be able to tag us! We waited and listened in silence trying to avoid getting caught. "Run! Run! Come on, this way!" Karen, a year younger than me, was always the athletic one but we both made it safely to the other side and the game began again.

We always liked it when Mary was available to play with us. She even played Cowboys and Indians.

Sometimes there were enough players to make a whole team of softball.

When we tired of games we would often visit our elderly neighbor and friend, Clara Meinkey. She was always a pleasant person to visit. She had a porch swing where we loved to sit and rest. Clara knitted or had a jig saw puzzle set up and our attention would fix on that.

Autumn presented another unique activity for us. We loved to play house. We created our own home out of the fallen leaves—a kitchen, living room, bathroom, and two bedrooms. The neighborhood boys could be such a nuisance. It was their mission to misbehave in our neat little world. They did not appreciate our unwritten rules that you could not jump walls. We had to chase those scamps away to keep them from messing up our house.

The winters were long and cold. Children were everywhere on days when the snow was right for sledding, snowball fights and building snowmen. I knew I could take my sled up town where two blocks of the steepest city street was off limits to cars. Bundled in snow pants and matching coat, snow boots, two or three pairs of socks, neck scarves tied in the back, knitted snow hats tied under our chins, two or three warm shirts, and double mittens, kids waddled down the streets pulling their dual-runner sleds by the rope attached to the guidance mechanism. There were sleds going down the hill and others being pulled back up the hill after their slippery descent. It didn't matter if you conversed with anyone. It was just great to be part of the fun.

It only took a few trips back up the steep hill before each child realized their toes and fingers were numb. I managed to slide my stiff fingers through the rope and pull the weightless sled back to the house for dry gloves and nourishment. The yummiest treat in the world was hot buttered toast dipped in hot cocoa and it was always on the menu after a fun day in the snow. I tugged on the gloves with my teeth to remove them from my red, icy fingers. Mom pulled my boots and socks off. The gloves and socks were draped on the back of a chair to warm and dry. My fingers and toes stung as circulation began to flow and feeling returned. After resting and warming, it was time to do it all over again but this time the sled stayed at home.

At the park kids were already busy building their snow forts—rolling huge balls of snow, packing them down into squares, stacking them up like huge bricks and rubbing them down with their mitten-clad hands to smooth them. As the snowballs flew it was like a western shoot-out. David was a good aim. One good splat from one of his missiles and I was ready to play something else. A trip to Kate Stoll's Drug Store provided a short rest stop. Two pieces of bubble gum for a penny or a Cherry Mash candy bar was a favorite treat. Soon we were tired and felt the chill come on again, this time being more of a chill from weariness. It was time to head to the house. But first we had to make a few snow angels. Karen and I fell backwards into the soft, plush snow, slid our arms and legs up and down a few times and then tried to get our padded bodies up without messing up our creations.

While the snow in the yard was still unspoiled, fox and goose trails were laid out and the neighborhood kids joined in the fun. Mary, my next door neighbor, was the "big" kid on the block, because she was older than the rest of us. She was the one who knew how to stomp out the trails. Karen, Cal, I and anyone else who happened to be in the neighborhood, joined in the fun. The fox chased the rest of us geese. As the fox chased us we ran squealing and giggling trying to avoid being tagged. We ran to the safe zone if we thought we were in danger but could only stay there a short time.

Christmas brought another cold weather treat. Santa arrived clad in his usual red suit, black boots and white cotton beard. Waving his arm atop the big red fire engine he exclaimed the traditional "Ho, Ho, Ho, Me-r-r-y Christmas"! He brought white paper sacks filled with hard candy, nuts and fruit for all the kids. After the kids received their gifts from Santa, the park filled with adults and children to anxiously await the drawing that was about to take place on the bandstand. For weeks everyone put their names in the boxes at the grocery stores. Now it was time to see who would get the prize—a bushel of groceries! The cold from the packed snow under our feet began to penetrate our boots. Rocking back and forth, stepping up and down, even though not going anywhere, would help keep the blood circulating to our toes.

At last the names were tossed and tumbled to make sure they were well mixed, and we heard the announcer, "Congratulations!" The name of a deserving family was announced. It was good the Christmas basket went to someone who needed it.

Finally it was over. At least I didn't have to walk two blocks home to warm up. Our little theater on the square, which was demolished this year, was showing cartoons all afternoon. It was not much warmer in there but getting out of the cold was definitely on our minds when we went in to watch and it did help. I rested and stayed close to the activities. As years passed the theater closed down and the movies were shown a few buildings away in the American Legion building. The only seating available there was hard, uncomfortable folding chairs. Eventually the Lutheran church opened its new addition and we walked one block off the square to watch *Scrooge*. I swear *Scrooge* was the only movie they ever showed! At least it was always playing when I went there.

One more trip to the square completed my day. Bailey and Jensen Variety Store always had so many interesting items. I wanted to find something nice to get Mom and Dad for Christmas. The store was stocked with the things kids love to see and hope to find under their tree on Christmas morning but I had to concentrate on finding a gift. Mom gave me some money to shop with but it was really hard to decide what to get. Finally I settled on a pretty, blue plastic napkin holder with tulips cut out on each side. That napkin holder sat on our kitchen table for many years.

CHAPTER SIX

Mary's mother had the most amazing player piano. She let the neighbor kids come in anytime and play it. To the right of the piano was a storage box with individual squares for each music roll. Mrs. Herr told me to be very careful with the rolls of perforated paper and I was. I opened the sliding doors on the front of the large, black walnut instrument, inserted the paper roll and pulled the pointed tab to connect it to the bottom roller, adjusted the settings just under the keys, placed my feet firmly on the floor pedals. Then with my hands tightly gripped under the keyboard for support, I pumped the pedals as hard as I could. "Roll out the barrel. We'll have a barrel of fun." That may not have been one of the songs. I don't know now but I did have my favorites and I loved the music.

Maybe that was why I mistakenly thought I should take piano lessons. For six long years I tried to become a pianist. Eventually I did learn to play some songs well – at least a few I liked – but the talent to be a pianist was not to be found in my fingers. On the other hand Cal was the pride and joy, not only of his parents and music teacher, but also of the town. After we performed in the annual recital I heard my parents' remarks on his extraordinary ability to play the piano—never heard much about mine though.

Other sounds of my childhood still rang in my mind. Red Rover, Red Rover, Send Candy Right Over. Bible school at the Methodist Church was fun. Play time was organized game time and Red Rover was a favorite. Everyone knew if Candy or I were summoned, we couldn't break the rope. I surveyed all the hands linked together and decided it didn't matter where I charged the lineup; I would wind up swinging from somebody's arm.

Cal knew his best vantage point was on the end. He locked both hands in a death grip on the kid next to him. He was small – a good target for someone who wanted to break through, but I guarantee he held on with enough fortitude and determination to keep the chain intact. Poor kid next to him probably wished Cal had a grip on someone else's hand. Maybe it was this determination that carried him so far through life, because it sure wasn't his exemplary behavior at church.

"Brighten the corner where you are. Brighten the corner where you are. Someone far from harbor you may guide across the bar. Brighten the corner where you are." Sunday was church day no matter where I was. If we went to visit out of town relatives

Mom and Dad had to find a church for me to attend. Cal had a perfect attendance pin. Every year he got to add another bar to it and I wanted one like his. Cal was always at church and his buddy and "partner in crime", David, was almost always beside him. They sat on the back row and Karen, Candy, Sherilyn, Judy and I sat on the next row. The most patient man in the world, Ham Sivadge, tried his best to teach us something but the girls were too busy whispering secrets and the boys were busy being boys. David was never at a loss when it came to making clever comments and Cal must have brought feathers from his pillow to church because we girls were always feeling something tickling our necks.

There was one Sunday Ham decided he had enough when the boys' antics were worse than usual. Two young gentlemen were excused for the remainder of the services but not before they had blamed their objectionable behavior on Keith, a quiet, obedient, reverent young fellow who decided that he might prefer to attend another church than to continue to be at the mercy of those rotten guys.

There was no taming the spirit in Cal and David. Dave was the innocent, poker-faced quipster and Cal was his over-appreciative audience. The first Sunday after being confirmed to join the Church was Communion Sunday. In those days we went up to kneel in the front of the Church along the railing while the minister, Rev Routh, brought the bread and wine—actually grape juice; we were Methodists. When Cal filed up and took his place he found his great friend, Dave on his left side. As luck would have it Ralph Wollenhaupt, the banker, came down from the Choir and took the spot on Cal's right side. Everything was fine, even though Rev Routh had Parkinson's disease and shook when he passed out the bread and said the communion words of instruction. Unfortunately Dave knew Cal's weaknesses for his humor and could not resist making an irreverent shaking impression which nearly caused Cal to break down. Cal bit his lip and made it through until the Reverend came back with the grape juice. David was ready. The boys had their eyes glued to the serving tray and as Ralph was served Dave leaned slightly toward Cal and whispered, "Ralph took two. "Cal started to chuckle and Dave knew Cal could not suppress through another absurd remark so he whispered again in his ever-consistent serious routine, "Cal, why did Ralph get two?" and Cal lost it. So there was Cal in front of the Church snickering, snorting and choking back laughter while his mother, the superintendent of the Sunday school, sat on the front row watching her only child in his big moment. And so it was all through our school days that those of us watching snickered first at David's comments that got him in trouble and then at the frustration of the adults who tried to deal with him.

For instance, the day some boys cut off a dead hawk's foot and left it on Marilyn's desk in typing class. Marilyn was the girl who squealed the loudest and I am sure that is exactly why her desk was selected for the special treat. Mr. Sawyer was the teacher. He was white haired and soft spoken but he stuttered whenever he spoke. "Who-who p-p-put that on Marilyn's desk," he asked angrily. "D-d-did you d-do that, David?"

"I don't know who did it. It wasn't me." David calmly and firmly avowed. With several siblings in his family I am sure he was very experienced in the art of getting out of and/or trying to stay out of trouble.

CHAPTER SEVEN

As the grade school years passed new kids moved to town. The girls usually became my best friends. It seemed the other kids already had their groups and interests. I wasn't athletic or a "groupie" so I seldom joined in a ball game or foot race. Besides I was accustomed to being alone most of the time since my brother was seven years older.

Joy was the one I remembered most from grade school. She was a year younger, but we had a great summer together. Although now living in Wisconsin, she visited me last year when I arrived back in Iowa. We talked about all the fun we had. In winter we slid down the frozen "gray" water runoff near the railroad bridge behind my house or played in my room. Sometimes we played in the park or went to her magnificently huge home. It was an older home but it was a mansion – maybe even three stories, with large white pillars on the front porch —a sight not often seen in farm country. It stood between two similarly built houses. Joy remembered playing softball with the other kids. Like me, she was not the athletic type. When it was her turn to bat, her nemesis, Craig, always had a snide comment for her. "Don't you need to go to the bathroom?"

"Speaking of bathrooms," she began, "Do you remember what we did in the restroom up town?" she asked. She was referring to the bandstand sitting in the middle of the park on the square. There were stairs on either side leading down to the restrooms.

"I remember the restrooms but I don't remember doing anything unusual there," I said wondering what in the world she remembered that I didn't.

"We went down there and wrote dirty words on the walls," she giggled.

"Are you sure? What did we write?" I couldn't remember anything about it.

"I don't know, but we did," Joy assured me.

"Are you sure you weren't with someone else?" I asked hoping I hadn't really done that wicked deed.

Just when I thought I knew every evil thing I ever did, along came Joy with a better memory than I. We had to have written language I heard from Dad like "Damn" or "Hell". I guess we blew off a little steam or maybe it was just an ornery streak coming out.

High school years were basically fun. I loved MYF meetings (Methodist Youth Fellowship). We sang fun songs during fellowship. The song about the Kookaburra was my favorite. I always thought it was about a donkey and couldn't figure out why he was in a tree. Traveling to other churches and meeting kids from other towns was great. It gave us a feeling of growing up—not being little kids.

One summer I told my parents I wanted to throw a party for my classmates. Mom was a trooper and helped me set up everything. We had plenty of hot dogs to grill and soft drinks for the evening. It was a beautiful day. Much to my surprise nearly everyone came. It was a great party. I felt really special that so many had come to MY house for a party. Mom and Dad made themselves scarce for the evening as I had asked them to, so I was in charge.

Everyone was eating and drinking and enjoying having a place to hang out. Cal and Beav (short for beaver and I don't know why he was called that. His real name was Steve) and two or three of the other guys were involved in hatching a plan. Why didn't we go ride around, get a Coke or something. It was just too much for me to resist. I was invited to join a group. It sounded like a great idea. Naïve me! It didn't dawn on me that being the only girl in the group. was not normal. Two of the guys crawled in the front seat and the remaining three of us in the back seat. I noticed Cal casually put his arm around my shoulders. Suddenly I had the feeling something was not right. Then it hit me. I had left my charge. I couldn't leave the house. It was my responsibility. We were about two blocks from home when I began wailing, "Take me home," I pleaded, knowing I was at their mercy. "Please," I begged. "I have to be there. It's my responsibility." I would have been in tears in a few seconds if the car had not turned and started back around the block to my house. There was not one person in that car that would have done an evil thing. It was just that I made a bad choice and had to correct it immediately.

I was home a few minutes after leaving but things had begun happening. One young fellow thought soft drinks might not be quenching his thirst and headed inside the house looking for a stash. He was sure to find his reward because Dad was known for his occasional "nips", but a couple of my responsible friends headed him off and no harm was done.

The remainder of the evening went well. My parents returned and everything was still intact. I decided that having the parents around would have been a much better choice.

CHAPTER EIGHT

The small town I was now eager to return to had not always been so dear to me. Memories of all those little things that went wrong and seemed big to me when I was young still plagued me. It took years to accept myself for who I was and put the foolish, childish things and adult shortcomings where they belonged – in the past. But it also took more than time to heal and feel that I was okay. I wondered if any of my friends had to deal with similar issues.

There were a couple incidents that involved Karen. I remember the day she and I each got a bottle of bubbles from the variety store. When we got back to the house I discovered I forgot to get the bubble blower. Since I didn't have one, I thought it reasonable that we could take turns using hers. She did not like that idea at all. Evidently the conversation got out of hand because Karen said she heard her mom calling her.

That couldn't be the end of that situation. I had a bottle of bubbles and no way to blow them.

Independent little snippet that I was, I just marched right back to the store and sneaked a bubble blower off the shelf and walked back home. When I returned home, Karen was in her yard and I was in mine. Mary's large yard was between us. We were a half a block apart; at least six houses besides our own were within spitting distance. I guess our mothers had told us to stay home so I stood on the edge of my yard and shouted to Karen who was standing at the edge of her yard, "I got my bubble blower!" I announced taunting her.

And Karen hollered back at me, "Where did you get it?"

I cupped my hands around my mouth as if that made the conversation more private and yelled as quietly as a yell can be, "I swiped it!"

"What," she called back.

A little louder, my hands still cupped, I replied, "I SWIPED IT!"

Mrs. Mangels, Mrs. Meinkey, Mr. and Mrs. Feick, Mr. and Mrs. Herr, Mrs. Reichardt, Mr. and Mrs. Queck, Mrs. Pruitt and my mom probably all knew by now I was a thief – but not a liar. Mom and I paid another trip to the variety store that day to straighten me out for stealing. I bet Mrs. Bailey would have given that stupid thing to me if I had just asked.

One day Karen announced she had a new baby sister. I really did not care about babies, but when baby Carol got old enough for Karen to push her in the stroller, I <u>really</u> did not like babies. I didn't want to play with a baby. I wanted Karen to play with me. I laughed and cruelly picked at Carol trying to make her cry, hoping Karen would get rid of her and come back to play with me but Carol was a good natured child and wasn't easily irritated. All I managed to do was irritate Karen and our friendship became a little strained.

Everyone makes poor choices occasionally but I made more than the average person. I had a stubborn determination and often thought that there was only one way to deal with a situation. Tact was not my strong point.

Case in point: Sometime before high school cheer leaders were chosen diplomatically, I was given a spot on the cheer leading team. That was fun – the travel, the uniforms, the practices and being a part of each sporting event. Our sponsor was a shriveled up old teacher who always looked like an angry little bull dog. She was a good teacher but scholastics were not my primary focus so I could not appreciate her good qualities.

One afternoon in the Home Ec. Room a few of us girls were trying on clothes and talking freely since we were fairly sure we were without adult supervision. Somehow the topic of the little bull dog came up and I said that I thought she was an old battle ax. The room went quiet. I was behind a dressing screen. It was not a pleasant surprise when the little bull dog poked her head around the screen and told me she thought I should return to class.

When I got home that evening, my parents were fully informed on the day's events and told me that I was no longer on the cheerleading squad. They told me the situation could be forgiven if I would just apologize. I was embarrassed, ashamed, angry and stubborn. I refused to apologize. Soon there were cheerleader tryouts for the entire squad and a new cheerleader sponsor. I missed it but not enough to admit I needed to change.

I continued to charge into life situations fully expecting the waters to part and found myself quite often running into concrete walls that didn't budge.

CHAPTER NINE

The high school years were finally over and at last I graduated in the class of 1964. Some kids took the summer off to just stay around home for a few months before delving into a more serious undertaking. NOT ME! I was anxious to get on with something—anything but living at home and staying in this town.

I had enough of being under my parents' rule, enough of those who thought they were better than me, enough of feeling not included, enough of being talked about. These things were, of course, my own skewed view of the world because of guilt and my self-condemnation for not being perfect and not always making right choices.

But now I could escape and go where nobody knew me or talked about me and do whatever I wanted. Business school began only a few weeks after graduation. Along with a few of my classmates I attended Omaha's Commercial Extension Business School in Omaha—Sandi with the dimples, cute smile and bubbly personality; Cousin Robert, who eventually worked with my dad in the quarry; Cal with the John Phillip Sousa award who loved to egg on a good joke, and Jeanie, my best friend. The trails of my classmates seldom crossed my path those days, or for many years to come, but the bond of growing up together always tied them to my heart. I didn't realize it until years later.

Jeanie was the new girl in town during my senior year and as usual, I adopted her as my best friend. She was a petite girl under five feet with short, bouncy, brown hair. She moved from Missouri, leaving a very difficult childhood behind, to live with her Uncle Vinton, our high school shop teacher. Jeanie also became my roommate at business school.

We moved into our "dorms". Ours was an old three-story house converted into bedrooms. There must have been 20 or more students living there. Jeanie was a lot like me in that she was always ready to laugh and have fun. And that is exactly what we did – had fun. Shopping and exploring were two of the ways we found to pass a long weekend in the city. One evening we rode the bus to the mall and I bought my very first two-piece swim suit. The light pink gingham suit was a long way from being a bikini, but I still felt exposed and uncomfortable in it. Another daring thing I did was to buy a neat mini skirt.

One weekend when we stayed in Omaha instead of going home, we spent a day walking to a mall and back. Just before we reached our dorm, a guy stopped to talk to us and then asked if we wanted to ride around. I said "No." But Jeanie decided to ride with him. She paid no attention to me when I tried to warn her of the danger she could be in. Jeanie jumped in the car, and to my amazement, dated Bill the rest of the time we were in business school, and married him after graduation!

Two specific memories I had about my time in Omaha were: 1) a popular song called *Downtown*, and 2) the night we missed the bus and had to walk back to the dorm.

Downtown was particularly appropriate because the theater was downtown, and "downtown" was really down hill all the way from the dorm. Jeanie and I decided to take the bus downtown to see a movie. We knew it would be close on catching the bus afterwards, but decided to take the chance. As we sat in the theater, it seemed the movie would never end. We were tensely watching the time. If we missed the bus we would probably not be able to get back to the dorm on time. We were so uneasy we got up out of our seats as the movie was getting near the finale. We slowly inched toward the door while trying to concentrate on the actors. I am sure neither of us could tell anyone how it ended. At the very moment the movie was over we ran out the theater doors to the bus stop but we were too late. The bus was on time that night and we missed it. There was nothing left to do but walk. It was quite a distance and it was definitely all uphill. We ran awhile and walked awhile. Curfew was not far away so we had to hurry as much as we could. Old Mrs. Rasmussin, the house mother, was not a pleasant person to get out of bed.

About half way back we saw a dark figure of a man coming toward us.

"Do you see that guy?" Jeanie whispered.

I knew by the way she said it there was something wrong. "Yeah," I whispered back.

"Just keep walking fast and cross over to the other side of the street."

"Okay." I trusted she knew something I didn't.

As soon as we were past the man, she grabbed my arm and said quietly, "Run."

I ran along with her until I had to catch my breath, "What's wrong?" I queried her.

"He was unzipped," she informed me.

"He what?" I asked not sure my ears had heard correctly. I wondered how she could see well enough in the darkened streets to notice that. At least we had each other for protection.

School went well. I graduated early and was eager to start working and earning my way. I was a good office worker and had no trouble finding a job. But as I continued to charge into life situations naively expecting sunshine and roses and happy endings, I found myself running into situations I didn't know how to handle. The wonderful innocent hometown atmosphere I had grown up in did not prepare me for reality pitfalls nor did I possess practical judgment.

My attitude about my home town only seemed to worsen as the years went by, and God knows it wasn't the town's fault. I knew it was the last place on earth I would ever return to. I was sure all the gossips and classmates had made the worst possible scenario of my life. When my parents were gone I would at last be done with not only that town, but the whole state.

Tumultuous relationships, self condemnation, and guilt all played their part in my withdrawing from everyone who had been a part of my childhood. Vacations were always spent driving to Mom and Dad's, staying three days, and seldom visiting any friends or family. Every one was always nice to me but I knew what they must say about my marriage track record. Things like, "Is that the same man she was with last time?" or "I wonder who she will bring next time?" or "How many husbands has she had?" I had to get to a point that it wasn't important what they said and accept myself.

CHAPTER TEN

Attending class reunions was definitely out of the question. My classmates lives all had to be better and more successful than mine. How could I face listening to all the success stories and seeing the happy marriages and pictures of beautiful children? Marriage and children were all I really wanted in life. Ten years after high school my accomplishments were two divorces and no children.

I always had excuses not to go to the reunions. For one thing, we never went to Iowa in May when the reunion was held. Every five years, I got a post card reminding me when and where the reunion was to be. One year I even got a personal phone call.

My phone rang and I answered, "Hello?"

"Hi, Valinda, this is Bob Welsch."

Oh, no. My mind reeled. This was a voice from my past, a classmate. I didn't want my life opened up to anyone I had ever known. "We are having our 30th class reunion next month and wanted to invite you to come."

"I don't think I will be able to come." I stumbled on my words and made some lame excuse.

I now had three failed marriages and was recently married to my fourth husband. At least I had slowed down on divorces – only one more in the twenty years since our 10ᵗʰ reunion. It wasn't likely that anyone else saw that as a positive. The third marriage was the longest and the worst even though I had tried so hard to make something go right. No one knew that except me and I could just imagine what they must think of me. I bet they get at good laugh at my expense. I couldn't face them. Thoughts just kept running through my mind. I had to get off the phone. "Well, it was nice talking to you, Bob." I said. He sounded disappointed as he gracefully said his goodbye.

I felt awful. It was the second time I had really botched a call requesting my attendance at a reunion.

Then one year during our vacation Robert and I were walking back to the house after browsing around the square during the Fourth celebration when I heard, "Valinda?"

"Yes," I said hesitantly looking into the face of a woman about my age but not being able to fit the features to anyone in my past.

"It's me, Karen," she said.

Something turned inside me. "Karen," I nearly cried. "My sandbox buddy! It is so good to see you." I hugged her with glee. "It's been so long." And the reminiscing began.

Karen met Robert and we visited. Robert has a deep non-threatening voice and can always say things that make people feel comfortable talking with him. His southern accent is captivating to a northerner's ear. The next year we saw Karen again. At last I had touched the past and it had not shaken me.

My fourth husband is a gem. As the years went by Robert's gentle manner helped me relax. Little things began to help change my outlook. He is the most patient, most honest, most loving person who has ever come into my life. With the same number of divorces in his past, he has plenty of reason to hold grudges but he never seems to let anything in his past cast a shadow on his attitude toward people. If he has a difficult situation to deal with he just waits until the right moment to handle it. I remember a time when a "friend" who owed Robert some money asked Robert to do something for him. It just seemed Robert never had the time to help him. In Robert's mind the score was settled. He has the tact, strength and stability I need in my life and has helped me change the mental image I held of myself.

Robert sealed the work that had already begun in my heart and mind many years before I met him. It was in Oklahoma that I found the benefits of attending church. I learned so many things that helped me overcome my stubbornness. I learned to be content in whatever state I was in. I even undertook reading the Bible all the way through. I am convinced that it contains all the wisdom a person needs. I read Fritz Ridenour's book on *How to be a Christian without being Religious*. This book did not contain new information but information that clarified and supported the Bible. I learned that when I prayed the primary focus was not on trying to convince God to do what I wanted but to mold my will to accept what His plan was for me no matter how difficult it seemed. I have to admit that I did not always act like I knew this information but the basic concepts were planted in my being for future reference.

CHAPTER ELEVEN

Soon it was time for my 40th class reunion. When I received the notice in the mail I actually started making plans to attend. It was going to be on the Fourth of July weekend. It was perfect timing. I was nervous but it was time for me to face up to the past and make the effort to rejoin. It was our 40th reunion and all 40 classmates were all still living.

Robert and I walked into the "Old Hotel" in Greenfield and stood in the unattended lobby wondering where to go. I was sure someone would rescue us in a very short time. At last Cynthia and Steve came in and led us to the room where the other classmates had congregated. I knew Steve right away. He was easy to recognize with the same amount of dark hair and only slightly heavier than I remembered. Many I could recognize easily but there were some whose faces took a little longer.

Ron was the greeter. He still looked much the same but his pretty red hair was now white with little to none on top. Bob had been a very curly, sandy blonde and he was also sporting the now popular hair color and style. Sherilyn was the same, Gene the same, Candy the same, Marilyn the same, Beverly the same, Sherry the same, Rex the same. The rest of us had to introduce ourselves.

I was so happy to see Sherilyn. She had a way of being nice to everyone and everyone liked her. Candy was another of my favorites and one who started school with me in kindergarten. There were twelve in our graduating class who started school together in kindergarten and nine of us were present at the reunion. Candy was the shortest of the class until Jeanie joined us in 12th grade. Like several of the girls, Candy had kept her figure and had changed so little.

And then it happened. The one person I hoped might not be there came into the room; the person who always managed to make me feel like the outsider. I quickly turned my back on her hoping she would not see me. Again my mind was racing. I actually caught myself wondering about places to hide – like under the table. This is foolish, I scolded myself. The room was not very large. I couldn't hide from her and I surely could not avoid her the whole evening. It would be nice if she felt the same about me and maybe we would not meet at all.

Get it together and get it over with, I told myself. Things are different now that we are adults. At last I took the initiative and walked up to her. "Hi girl," I greeted her with all the enthusiasm I could muster, "It is so good to see you again."

She was totally gracious and introduced me to another classmate she was standing next to. We visited a few minutes until we were distracted by other conversations. Wow, was I glad that was over; now I could get through the rest of the evening. What a relief it was to finally realize how foolish it was to allow the petty, old, negative childhood memories to taint my view of the present.

We seated ourselves at the tables to be served. The food was not great that night but I managed to eat enough to ward off hunger pains. I turned to my right and there she was again. I was not the reason she was there. I was sure of that. She was heavily engaged in conversation with someone across the table from me. Then she took me by surprise when she turned to me and said, "I was always so jealous of you."

I was totally taken aback, "That's hard to believe! You were so popular and the homecoming queen. How could you be jealous of me?"

"You had all the things I didn't. You had a job and your own money to spend. You had a figure that made your clothes fit right. I was so thin that everything hung on me. The guys all thought you were so pretty and your folks were always there for you," she told me. She had just confided the reason for her behavior in school.

Confession and confronting had been one of my strong points to put right a past relationship. She had stolen my "thunder", and I was glad she had. At least now I had information to help me understand why our long-ago connection always had a broken link. Evidently she had also learned that facing issues was the best way to take away the unpleasant memories and mend unhealthy situation.

The reunion evening drew to a close and it was picture time. I grabbed up my friend, Candy, and sat with her on the front row. Behind me I felt an irritating, faintly familiar tickle on my neck. I turned around and saw Cal. I should have known. "You used to do that to me in Sunday school class when we were kids," I said. It was a memory that would never have come back to me otherwise. He just grinned knowing we connected again after all these years.

The reunion was over and I survived. The pains of being a hard-headed, independent child finally eased. The past was now mostly where it belonged—in the past. Although I still had few things to deal with the worst was behind me. The past was no longer important – kaput.

I began email communications with several classmates which proved to be the final step in accepting myself. One classmate in particular began asking questions about my past. It was not important whether the questions stemmed from curiosity or concern, or both. I began writing replies that no doubt gave more detail than they expected or wanted but I found great benefit in doing it. It was not even important that the things I talked about might not remain "just between us," because as I finished writing each episode, I found that I felt relieved. Someone finally knew what I knew. I became bold enough to joke about my past and realize that everyone has one (a past) and each person has to choose how to deal with it. If someone mentioned something about a person being married XX number of times I might say something like, "They are going to catch up with me." I could now return to my home. The past no longer had a grip on my emotions

CHAPTER TWELVE

I really did not want Dad to see us bringing our things into the house so each item was quickly whisked up the stairs while he was away from the house and before he had a chance to interject his questioning criticism of every move I made. The two bedrooms were crowded but organized. At last we were settled into our rooms. Dad had not invited us to stay with him and I am sure he considered this extra company an imposition of his privacy. That fact by itself probably accounted for several of his outrages.

Dad was a feisty fellow in his younger days. His frame was small but sturdy standing about 5 feet 8 inches. He spent his military service in the Navy as a fireman/engineer on a ship called the Queens 103. "The Queens was 400 feet and one inch long," Dad told me when I asked him about his military stint in the Navy. The details were still fresh in his mind. He was so talented with engines and equipment, he could fix nearly anything and he wasn't satisfied unless it was done right. When Dad did something, it had to be precise – even if he had to call on his friends, "Gawd Damn" and "Je-s-u-s Christ", to help. "Son of a Bitch" and "That Bastard" usually got in the way—but Dad always got it done.

When Dad reminisced about his military duty he told me his ship was sent to Iwo Jima where 28 small boats, called LCVPs (Landing Craft Vehicle Personnel) were launched beside the ship. Only seven or eight ground soldiers with full combat gear could fit into each boat. The men climbed down a net lowered over the side of the ship to board the small boats. Dad was one of the men in charge of taking the soldiers close to shore where a ramp was lowered for the men to disembark. He saw men die as boats were bombed by enemy aircraft before they reached their destination. He knew the risk he faced each time he made his run.

He sat quietly for a few moments and then he spoke softly, "After each battle we went ashore to undress the soldiers who died. We placed blankets over their bodies," he told me almost without emotion—a heart-wrenching fact of war few of us knows about. "The clothes were taken back to the ship to be sanitized and redistributed."

He told me a story about one the events that lifted their spirits. It was about the bomber planes and their victory dance. The soldiers took control of a short landing strip at the base of Mt. Suribachi. The American bombers, which were called Mustangs, took off from Mt. Suribachi to combat the enemy craft called Zeros. If the Mustangs were successful in taking out an enemy plane, they zoomed up the side of Mt. Suribachi before landing to announce a victory flight to the onlookers on ship and land. I can almost feel the adrenalin rush the soldiers must have felt knowing their comrades did well and came back safely. It was atop this mountain six men raised our flag on Iwo Jima.

I am proud Dad fought in World War II and was part of *"The Greatest Generation."*

After the military, Dad worked on construction jobs; one in Iceland, and later, another in Trinidad. He returned to the states upon receiving notification his father was hospitalized with a cerebral hemorrhage. I was about six years old, my brother 13. I remembered standing outside the hospital waving to Grandpa in his second story hospital room. Children my age were not allowed on the patient floor. Thankfully, Dad spent a few days with Grandpa Jay before he died.

Dad then worked for Schildberg Construction when the company was new and struggling. They appreciated Dad's adept abilities in running equipment, acute attention to detail, and his lack of tolerance for poorly done jobs. He was appointed supervisor over a rock-crushing crew. This was the last job he held. After he retired, he continued to work occasionally for Schildbergs until he was in his seventies.

He may have retired but he did not change. His stubborn determination and gritty attitude was well intact.

The first thing I absolutely had to do was get internet service. The house had not changed in the twenty-two years since Mom died and was outdated. It was like walking into a scene from the sixties. Dad didn't want the living room (or anything else) changed but he finally decided to allow me to have my computer upstairs. A phone line had to be put in. Money was a big issue so I sent a check to the phone company to pay for the extra expenses before the bill came in. He told me years ago that if he couldn't take his money with him, he wasn't going. I was beginning to think that he was more serious about that than anyone could have thought. The phone line installation went well and I hoped that we would continue to come to terms with other issues as easily, but I soon found out that this was a small battle compared to others that would follow.

As soon as the phone bills started coming in with the internet charges there was a new issue to face. At first I gave him cash for the additional charges for internet service but that did not suit him. He wanted me to get internet billed separately. Time and time again I told him there was no way to separate the phone bill from the internet charges. I finally lost my patience and firmly stated, "We have already gone over this several times and agreed on what has to be done."

He always had a comeback I wasn't expecting. "Well if we have already settled this, why are we still discussing it," he said with complete calmness. I just let out a deep breath and walked away. In a few minutes he came back to the kitchen where I was preparing supper and got the best of me again. "Since you are in charge of my business now, where is my hat?" He did have a sense of humor but I didn't usually appreciate it.

CHAPTER THIRTEEN

Now that I was "home" again, I fell into old routines and habits, the things my mother did when I was young, just as naturally as if I had never left. I found hanging clothes on the line was almost fun; doing dishes by hand was not but it only took a few minutes. There was no leaving the dishes until later. Dad expected certain things to be done at certain times and adjusting his schedule was not optional. I prepared meals three times a day. He showed up for lunch at 12:00 and supper at 5:00. He didn't need to be called to eat. He was just there like when Mom was alive.

I noticed some days were more complicated than others for Dad. Normally, he placed the correct things on the table, but other days it was difficult for him to determine what was appropriate. I called those "fuzzy days", when his mind seemed less sharp.

His nights were not any better. Every night Dad went through everything. The kitchen was his favorite "haunt." I washed the dishes after supper and left them draining on the counter. By morning the dishes were put away. He went through every drawer and door in the cupboards mentally inventorying every detail there and in the refrigerator to make sure it was still in order. Whatever I put in the refrigerator was inspected before morning. If the seal was broken on a package of meat that came from the fresh meat counter at the grocery store, I found a rubber band around it. If a bag of vegetables in the freezer was opened and partially used, a rubber band was around them as well. Organization was paramount. The butter sat on top of the eggs, the bread on the right side of the second shelf, his little bowl sat on the left side fourth shelf, etc. etc. If anything was moved in the house, he noticed it. If only one thing was out of place he told me "everything" was messed up. I wondered if this could be attributed to dementia or was this just his normal over-attention to detail.

The first few nights I heard his meddling around but soon I was too tired to notice and slept through his nightly escapades. The next morning I heard a list of things he found out of order. For instance:

"I couldn't find the ketchup."

"Where did you get those white bowls? I couldn't find a place to put them in the cupboard."

"The drawer with the plastic bowls (butter bowls and cool whip bowls) is all messed up."

It was such a constant struggle to keep things exactly where he wanted them that I spent all my free time in my room where I felt least exposed to his scrutiny and where I did not have to worry about disturbing his nest. I was perfectly content to play internet games or take naps; but Dad was not happy when I was not in his company. He wanted constant companionship like he had with Mom.

Spending time with him was monotonous. I heard the same subjects over and over again, like the earrings made on the sidewalk in Trinidad or things he liked to argue about. He took great delight in useless and senseless "debates", as he called them, and I had not learned the game strategy. Dad always ruled. Mom had always dealt with him in the past. I was the quiet, obedient little girl who didn't make waves. I remembered the arguments I heard in the kitchen below my bedroom and wished they would stop. Mom was gone now and he now turned his overbearing demands toward me. I was determined not to become victimized by his behavior but, it took time to learn proper responses to ward off the attacks.

Although he never came right out and said it, I knew he was suspicious of my motives for moving in with him. He treated me like an unwelcome house guest at times—someone who wanted to rob him blind. My goal was to make life easier for him. I thought he would be grateful for my efforts to help him maintain the lifestyle he was accustomed to. How wrong I was.

Robert and I planned to take over payment of the utility bills as soon as he retired and we no longer had the cost of maintaining a separate household in Arkansas. In the interim, I would pay any extra costs incurred while staying with Dad. I thought our help was something Dad would welcome. After all, he didn't have to consider living in a nursing home that would cost him several thousand dollars a month. Instead, he thought that he was doing us a favor by letting us live in his house. He decided that I should buy all the groceries and pay all the utilities right away. I thought this was another attempt to try to get us out of his house. What I had not realized yet was that the situation was more like a spider/fly relationship. I walked into his web voluntarily. He had me trapped and would now work on me from every direction until he could to get things the way he wanted them. I was always a push-over and it felt like he was sucking the life out of me. When I broached the subject of getting another place to live, that was not the solution he was looking for.

CHAPTER FOURTEEN

Since my retirement, I was afforded the pleasure of lying in bed until I was ready to get up – at least on weekends. Robert was very good about fixing himself whatever he needed before leaving for work. He not only got up by 5:30 to prepare his own breakfast, but also arrived at work at least 15 minutes early. Often he brought me a cup of coffee or my usual peanut butter and toast breakfast before leaving.

Deborah got up about 6:30. I fixed her breakfast, saw that she had her teeth brushed and was on the bus by 7:20. Then I would spend the rest of the day as I pleased. On days when I felt bad, she took care of everything without help. My family had me spoiled. Getting unspoiled was a difficult task but my Dad was definitely up to the challenge. Being in my father's house was not nearly as pleasant as I had hoped.

In the mornings Dad set the table and got the necessary items out of the refrigerator before I got up. Sometimes he had leftovers from the previous night's meal on the table along with his famous little bowl. This bowl, a Cool Whip container, which always had 4 things in it – round, sliced, smoked turkey lunch meat cut in quarters, baby carrots, pieces of onion and a wiener. If something was left over from a previous meal, he added it to the bowl. It was alarming to see limp soggy French fries and a piece of hamburger or some other unrecognizable leftover come out of it.

Occasionally I removed the dried, shriveled carrots from the bowl and replaced them with fresh ones. At the same time, I either washed the bowl out or replaced it with a fresh bowl, being very carful to replace it with exactly the same type of container so he did not get confused or suspicious of the change.

At first I managed pretty well, but as the days wore on, I found it increasingly difficult to meet his expectations. With the emotional drain of dealing with his moods I became tired and weary. I did not even get weekends off—seven days a week, every week, clad in my pajamas and my hair just barely brushed, I dragged my exhausted body down the stairs to the kitchen at precisely 6:30 after being summoned by Dad, the Lord of the Kitchen.

"You up there?" he asked standing beside the open stairway.

Where else would I be? I thought. "Yes Dad," I wearily replied.

I again hear his voice, "You ready to come eat breakfast?"

"I'm awfully tired this morning," I told him, hoping for a little mercy.

"You are lazy. Am I going to have to come drag you out of that bed?" he threatened.

"Yeah, come on," I calmly responded, wondering just how far he was going push this.

I lost. He didn't come up the stairs but I knew waging this war was more trouble than surrendering.

Breakfast was over, dishes were done and now it was nap time. I had to get caught up on my rest. I lay down on the bed and in no more than five minutes I heard his voice again. "Are you asleep?"

I'll just play possum, I thought, and did not answer. After all if I am asleep, how can I answer? "Are you awake?" he called a little louder. Obviously he wasn't interested in how tired I was or if I was asleep, and did not intend to be ignored.

Tromp, tromp, tromp, I heard his slow footsteps coming up the stairs. Playing possum was not working but I was not giving up yet. He stood directly over my head and shouted. "ARE YOU ASLEEP?"

No longer could I contain the absurdity of the situation and broke out in laughter. Totally angered by now and not expecting the reaction he got, he stomped off in disgust, "By gawd when I ask a question, I expect an answer!" At last I got a little rest.

I decided I had to make myself wake up before he called me. Maybe that would take the edge off. I set the radio alarm for 6:00, my telephone alarm at 6:15 and asked my husband to call about 10 minutes after the alarms to make sure I was awake. Even then I lay in the bed until I could hear Dad scuffling around below me in the kitchen before I got up.

The arguing and unpredictable moods worsened. The thought occurred to me again that he didn't want me in the house at all. "Dad, I don't have to live here, I said. Robert and I can buy a house, but that will mean we will be spending time taking care of our place." I probed him for an acceptable resolution but he was increasingly vague. He knew if we moved he would lose control. His frustration grew at not being able to dominate me in his own home. He had a tremendous dilemma. He was not accustomed to not getting what he wanted but he eventually conceded in vague expressions that he wanted me to stay where I was. The subject was temporarily closed until he could come at me again.

CHAPTER FIFTEEN

Before I came, Dad had supper with Marsha every Tuesday night, but he always waited for Marsha's call to invite him to eat. She had done this for him ever since Mom died over twenty years ago. One evening Marsha prepared a meal from one of Mom's recipes and thought Dad might really enjoy it. The meal was ready but Dad didn't come. "Now that is strange," she remarked to my brother, Delano, as she looked out the window. To her surprise she saw Dad's car passing about a block away. "Oh, no," she exclaimed. "I forgot to invite him!" Delano looked for him but Dad had evidently left town.

Marsha is now alone. Delano died five years ago and she became a great companion for me. She loves to go to the horse races and spend a little time in the casino. I just wished she had taken me to the races the day she met Mario Lopez. I would not have known who he was either. It was the day after the races when she finally realized who had been talking to her.

Marilyn, a classmate and friend, was another person who helped me keep my sanity. She moved back to Fontanelle a few months after my move. Leaving behind friends, activities and much busier communities, we both occasionally felt a little isolated. As classmates we already knew we had similar personalities and it was such fun to rekindle our friendship.

Marilyn, who once had a private investigator's license, and I made weekly road trips to "investigate" available resources in nearby communities with emphasis on places to eat lunch for a really great price. There was not a secondhand store, flea market or junk store that could escape our scrutiny.

It was not long before we gave each other nicknames. One day I called her up on the phone and she answered, "Hello."

"Hello," I responded in a heavy nasal disguise. "Is this Grump Butt?" a name I had given her because she said she got grumpy when she got tired.

Marilyn, always quick on the draw and ready for a good laugh, replied emphatically in a similar masquerade, "No it is not. This is Dragon Butt."

"I'm sorry. I must have the wrong number," I concluded.

"Cheeky? Is that you," she asked in fake surprise.

We both laughed and continued a normal conversation—at least what was normal for us. She likes to call me cheeky girl because I am so mischievous and outspoken. She eventually began calling us the "Mafia Mommas". She thought that our unpredictable behavior terrorized the shopping districts.

It was Marsha and Marilyn who gave me outlets to take time to laugh, so that when things were difficult at home I was relaxed enough to handle the situations.

CHAPTER SIXTEEN

Some incidents with Dad were minor like the day I had about three small dishes to wash. I thought they were hidden under the inverted dish pan in the sink and went back upstairs to take a nap. It wasn't long before I heard noises in the kitchen. Dad found them and was sort of slamming the plastic 1950s Melamine plates and eating utensils around as he washed them and put them away. Not only did he convince me he didn't appreciate my slovenly ways, but I discovered I didn't want him doing the dishes his way! His way consisted of his finger and running water.

"There are purifiers in the water," he told me.

"Plain water will not get the scum off." I tried to make him understand.

"Oh a little scum won't hurt me," he said.

Actually he just didn't want to spend any money buying the soap to wash them with.

At times there were childlike qualities to him that reminded me of a little boy. One day while bringing in laundry from the line, a tiny toad hopped into the garage just as I closed the door. Knowing Deborah was a little down, I decided to put it in a bucket and take it up to show her. Dad saw me with it and had to check it out.

"What are you going to do with it?"

"I'm taking it to show Deb," I told him.

"Don't hurt it," he said.

"I won't," I promised.

Again and again he had to know what I was doing with the toad.

"He's kind of tame. I touched him and he didn't move," Dad said reflecting on the little fellow.

"Of course he didn't move. There isn't enough room in the bowl he's in." I put the toad in an ice cream bucket and gave him a few leaves and a couple sticks to climb on.

"Where are you going with that bucket?" he demanded.

"I just want to show him to Deb."

"Don't leave him up there."

"I won't."

"Don't hurt him."

"I won't."

"He needs to be outside where he came from. Anything else would be mean."

"I'll put him back outside."

"Put him over by those horse radish plants," he instructed.

"OK."

I showed the toad to Deb, and she had a little fun checking him out. Then I took him back out and put him by the horse radish plants.

"Where's the frog?" Dad had to know immediately.

"I put him in the horse radish plants."

"Where did you find him?" He asked and I told him again. "You probably should have put him back where you found him. He is awfully little. He might be lost."

I just knew the next thing he wanted me to do was find the frog and take the "little fellow" and back to the garage. I was thankful he didn't pursue that.

His childish behavior was a little embarrassing in the doctors' offices when he would shoot a constant stream of questions.

Dad complained often of a cough and drainage in his throat. We sat in the doctor's office waiting to be seen. He saw the doctor, went upstairs for x-rays and came back downstairs to wait for the results. Dr. Thompson had an emergency call so the wait was getting tedious. We sat in a clinic room where Dad incessantly questioned me with things I could not answer. It reminded me of Deborah's questions. "When will Dr. Thompson get here?" "What is she doing?" What kind of emergency was it?" "How long will it be?"

"I don't know but I'll go ask, Dad. You wait here." I told him and escaped his questions with the only excuse I could think of.

I wasn't to get off that easy. He wasn't going to sit in that clinic room by himself. He was about ten paces behind me. We decided to continue our wait in the waiting room.

"What did they say?" It was starting again.

"She will be here as soon as she can," I told him.

In minutes he was at it again. "How much longer?" he asked.

"If you want to go up to the desk and pester them go right ahead. I'm not going to do it." He sat quietly pondering what to do for a few seconds before he was on his feet. By this time our whispers had reached the ears of others in the waiting room and I could see their amusement.

Dad settled back in his chair but he wasn't through with his capers. Earlier he had gotten a sample of his sputum on a paper towel while he was in the bathroom and he delighted in showing it to me. "It is okay, Dad," I said sounding as bored as possible hoping he would drop the subject.

He sat there holding the paper towel in both hands between his knees. Then, to my horror, he dropped it on the floor. "Dad, pick that up!" I softly demanded as if I were scolding a child.

"I got tired of holding it," he said.

"Put it in your pocket." I couldn't believe he was behaving like a bored child.

His mood could change drastically and did when a part on the washing machine broke. Seems I always managed to say some innocent comment that set him off and he started yelling at me. This was one of those times I couldn't reason with him.

I turned on my heel and started for the door. "I'll be back in a little while when you have calmed down," I told him.

"Don't you walk away from me!" he demanded. I tried to keep on going but I just couldn't. He was my Dad and I had always obeyed. I stopped in my tracks and silently stood by his side while he removed the lid. That's right, the whole lid to the washing machine! He was taking it to the store to get a new part. The lid did not contain any information that the store needed so I silently wrote down the model and serial numbers. I couldn't believe he walked in the store with the lid. An even greater surprise was when the plumbing store employees were so professional and kept straight faces. They allowed Dad to maintain his dignity. I slipped the piece of paper with the serial number to the lady and in a few days we had the needed part.

CHAPTER SEVENTEEN

Two years ago during our usual vacation to Iowa, Deb made a friend. We attended Uncle James' 99th birthday celebration in his home town of Bridgewater, a town even smaller than Fontanelle, about five miles west of Fontanelle. He was more active and alert than Dad. James continued to make daily trips to the farm even after his wife, Aunt Lena, died. His son, Marlin, farmed the family farm and they often discussed progress and problems and James made recommendations. James' two sons and three grandsons and their wives decided at the last minute to celebrate his 99th birthday with an open-house card shower and refreshments. That was a providential choice. They had a wonderful turnout. Uncle James suffered a stroke a few months after the birthday party and died a short time before his 100th birthday.

It was there at the open-house that Deb met Candys. (Creative spelling of Candice) Now they could renew their friendship. Candys was such a vivacious, energetic and friendly child. They were quite a pair—Candys with her long hair in dog ears and Deb with her pony tail.   I took Deb swimming and Candys was there.   I took Deb to the Fourth of July fireworks display and Candys was there. At each discovery they were together again, they took each others hands and bounced with glee at having another opportunity to play together.

Our first summer as residents of Iowa was exhilarating - more than either of us anticipated. In June we traveled to the massive Omaha Zoo for an all-day outing with Aunt Susie and her family. Candys' family took Deb to the Adventure Land Amusement Park east of Des Moines in July. At home she was free to roam the town just as I had as a child. Many afternoons found the "town" kids at the ceramics shop on the square engrossed in painting a figurine of their choice.   During harvest time, Uncle Marlin let Deb ride with him while he harvested corn. The enormous machine ran its metal fingers between the rows of corn pulling ears, shucking and shelling and spitting out everything but the kernels which went into the holding bin. When the holding bin was full, the snout sticking up in the air augured all the kernels into a wagon that would carry the corn to the local elevator for storage.

The excitement for me was discovering the positive attributes of small town life that I had not appreciated in the past. I just couldn't soak up enough of the views of green crops growing, the fresh air and the friendly atmosphere. Everywhere I went, whether it was taking the dog to the vet, establishing our medical care or having my car's oil changed, I met people who were adept at their occupations.

Fontanelle and Greenfield were neat little towns with manicured lawns, curbed streets, and sidewalks almost everywhere. As a matter of fact, Greenfield was so neat that if one's lawnmower blew grass on the city streets, a visit from one of the cities finest most certainly was in the owner's immediate future.

Greenfield's 1,888 citizens learned their versatile police force could be depended upon for any emergency. They were called not only for the numerous medical emergencies but also for this call:

> 2:00 p.m. Friday, Chief O. and off-duty Officer H. located an intoxicated person lying on the sidewalk (in the afternoon?) on the south section of the Public Square. The subject lived three blocks from the location and was transported to his residence.

> They were frequently called out for livestock on the road. Maybe this is why so many people thought they should consider them animal control managers as well.

Monday, August 3

Raccoon in building at the eastbound Adair rest area

Wednesday, August 5

Animal welfare call

September 17

Officer H. was dispatched to the Public Square because a duck was under a motor vehicle. The duck left the area of the parked cars.

September 21

Chief O. was notified of a duck in the city swimming pool. The chief and a city worker removed the duck and later released it at the Greenfield Lake.

September 19

Officer L. was called to the 400 block of South First Street in regard to a snake in the road. The subject who called in the complaint took care of the snake.

You call the police for a snake in the road? I thought you were just supposed to scream and get the hoe.

It was our privilege to read all of these episodes in the Greenfield Free Press each week so everyone could play guessing games as to who was involved in each incident. Names may not have been mentioned but locations were. It made quite stimulating conversation at some of the local retirement gatherings.

The officers were adept at managing disputes:

> Chief O. came upon five retired male subjects at the corner of SW Jackson and 3rd Streets. The subjects were getting kind of loud and the neighbors could hear the disturbance. Chief O. approached the subjects standing on the sidewalk and asked them to hold the noise down. One male subject attempted to show his back half until Chief O. took out his citation book and dared him to do so. Apparently the discussion was over the current federal administration on health care. After a friendly conversation with the male subjects, the gathering returned to normal.

> #

> Officer L. was dispatched to the location of the 300 block of N.W. Grant Street in regard to a domestic situation between a female and a male subject. The

male subject alleged the female had assaulted him. The officer could not see any physical evidence an assault had occurred. No arrests were made. (Hmmm. No blood, no knife, no gun, no frying pan. No problem)

#

Officer H. took a report and complaint of harassment from a citizen in the 200 block of N.W. 2nd street. The complaint stated he was getting harassing text message from another male subject. (I wonder how old he was—maybe 9 or 10.)

#

Officer H. was called to the location of the Greenfield Park Apartments in regard to a disturbance between a male and female subject. Apparently the female came to the apartment and kicked in the door. (Mean woman!) The apartment belonged to the female. The officer attempted to locate the female subject but could not find her. (He was probably glad.)

#

Officer H. observed two vehicles driving recklessly on   the Public Square. The subjects in both vehicles had been shouting profane words towards each other.   The parties involved were advised to go home and stop harassing each other.

#

Chief O. was dispatched to the location of the apartment complex on NW 2nd Street in regard to a domestic disturbance.   Upon arrival it was discovered both parties were arguing with each other.   The individuals were advised to stop the disturbance in the apartment complex.   (Just cut that out!)

#

These surely were the most patient public servants on earth.   One week Officer L. was sent to investigate someone "messing around" on the highway.   Poor fellow, he never did find that person. Many other times "wild goose chase" probably described best what they were feeling:

Saturday, August 8

Officer H. was advised of a drunk driver heading south on Lakeview Drive.   Upon arrival at the location the vehicle had already left the area and could not be found.

#

Officer L. was dispatched to the area of the swimming pool in reference to a complaint of a vehicle driving recklessly. The officer located the vehicle a short time later parked at an apartment complex. (Guess he just went back to the office.)

Wonder how often they got calls like this one:

11:05 p.m. Officer H. had a report of a subject pounding on the walls at the location of the senior apartments on Nobel Street. Upon arrival the officer was advised the person was hanging something on the wall.

#

There was not a single traffic signal in the entire county except for one flashing amber light. Speed limits were well-respected and I think I know why. My Aunt was driving through Greenfield on the main highway, speed limit 25. She saw a radar marker clocked her at 27 mph but did not give it a second thought. Before she completed her twelve-block journey, she was in possession of a warning ticket.

Community involvement was amazing. There were so many things to do. For instance on Halloween "Scary Prairie" was advertised in the Greenfield Free Press as:

A different Kind of Halloween Fright

Thrill seekers can prowl through TEN acres of tall prairie grass during "Scary Prairie" on Thursday, Friday, and Saturday, October 15 - 17 from 6 to 9 pm at the Henry A. Wallace Country Life Center, 2773 290th Street, Orient, IA. Under the light of a half moon, the eerie sounds of howling coyotes, running deer, rustling badgers and "things that go bump in the night" are sure to provide plenty of yells and screams. Participants can make their own s'mores over an open fire as they watch for the ghosts that inhabit the prairie. Scary Prairie is recommended for ages 8 and older. Flashlights and identification badges are issued to all to be turned in upon safe return.

#

Far out in the country was this wonderful community center built as a tribute to Henry A. Wallace, the 33rd vice president of the United States, 11th secretary of agriculture, 10th secretary of commerce, and a man termed by a reporter as Iowa's greatest son. I took Deb to this event. The weather was threatening rain and they did not have a good turnout. I wondered what wandering through a prairie could be like; how could they find all the kids when it was over? Did they just wander around in tall grass and look for scary things? We found that mowers cut trails for the kids to follow and "scare" points were set up along the way. She had such a good time she went through it three times. We went back the following night and took Candys with us.

CHAPTER EIGHTEEN

Even though Dad was a constant challenge the summer was great for me also. Due to his most recent accident where he hit the two parked cars, he received a notice that he would be required to take the written and driving tests in order to keep his license. That was good news to me because I was hoping that he would not pass the test.

He stormed and fussed about it but he studied hard. "I don't understand why they think I need to take this test again."

"Maybe they don't understand why you hit those cars." I foolishly tried to reason with him. "You weren't really picking up the phone book when you hit those cars were you?"

"What makes you say that," he asked after hesitating and shooting a couple of suspicious glances my way.

"You said that was what 'you told the Officer'. You <u>didn't</u> say it was what you <u>did</u>," I challenged him.

He stammered a bit and finally said, "I guess I was looking away—toward the beauty shop."

"I think you looked away alright. I think you went to sleep." He didn't offer any argument and the subject was dropped. When the subject came up again, he did not remember admitting he had not picked up the phone book. Hmmm that must be selective memory.

He had a month to study. This was quite stressful for him. At last the time came for him to take the written test. Surely, he will fail it, I thought, and the problem with driving will not be a problem anymore. No, Dad wasn't going to fail. Driving was too important to him. It was the one thing he could do to pass time away that did not require a lot of effort. He studied and pondered each question and answer until it made sense to him. He had me ask him the questions to see if he could get them right.

He failed the written section the first time but he went back the next day and passed it. The driving test was not nearly as difficult for him as the written part. Now were back to square one. Dad was still driving.

CHAPTER NINETEEN

Dad liked to be busy but there were not many things for a man his age to do. Driving was the one thing he enjoyed. It was not unusual for him to get in his car half a dozen times a day and drive around town or out to the cemetery. He missed Mom a lot, but his most recent heartache was that his son, my sweet brother, Delano, was now there. Cancer took him five years ago. "He shouldn't be out there on that hill," he often lamented.

Delano was seven years older than I. We never managed to establish a close relationship until the day we connected by email. He loved that mode of communication as much as I.

When we were children we liked to play behind our house near the train tracks. The train, called the Cumberland Rose, ran on tracks that ran in a man-made gulley. Dirt that had been removed from the track area was piled up on our side of the tracks making a very unkempt mound of dirt all along the edge of our yard. It was uneven, weedy, and generally a wilderness of adventure for kids. I followed Paul, Karen's older brother, and Delano up there one day just because I wanted to see if they would let me play with them, but I wasn't welcome. Delano was not one to waste words or actions. He simply picked up a nasty, dirty worm and put it in my hair. I went screaming and crying back to the house. Somehow Mom seemed to think I had some things coming and I didn't get any more sympathy than a hair wash.

She may have been remembering the day Delano took one of my toys away from me. I was probably no more than two. Of course I don't remember the incident. That was when Dad was building onto our house and there were pieces of lumber and nails lying around. I picked up a piece of two-by-four and landed it on Delano's head. Mom and Dad seemed to think he had that coming so I guess we got treated pretty much the same.

Even though Fontanelle was a smaller town than Greenfield with a population of only 813 in its prime, it was full of businesses in the 50s and 60s. On the square were two pharmacies, three nice busy groceries stores, one not-so-busy grocery store, a bank, a barber shop, a post office, a theater, a dry cleaners, two taverns, a variety store, a hardware store, 2 or three cafes, a furniture store, City Hall, doctor's office, a feed store, an American Legion building, newspaper office, a library and three gas stations. We loved to buy fresh roasted peanuts from Frankie Rice's peanut and popcorn stand. On Wednesday and Friday nights we could get snow cones.

Delano owned the D-X Gas Station a block west of the south side of the square. It sat on the North side of the road. On the south side, directly across from the station, was the Fontanelle water tower with a little red light on top.

Delano may have been a man of few words but he was a man of many talents. Primarily he was a Cracker Jack mechanic and that drew many of the teens to his station for help on their older model cars. In those days teenagers seldom drove new cars. This was the era of classic cars like the '57 Chevy and '58 Ford convertibles. It was such fun to customize an old car. Cal's first car was nearly new – a Black, Chevy Impala 2-door hardtop. Of course sound was always important so Delano helped him put in a rear seat speaker. Dual exhausts that sounded sweet were the next item on the list of things a car had to have.

Delano's modifications were not always standard or sensible. His creativity went far, way far, beyond what any other mechanic would consider. One of his delights was to confound the lawmen. Somehow he came up with an idea to put two, very illegal 100 watt airplane landing lights in the head lights. Talk about bright. Some of the UFO sightings in those days were probably in reality Cal's '60 Chevy.

When Cal came onto the North side of the square in Greenfield he flashed his high beams and the city street lights shut down. The police would start racing around trying to figure out what caused the lights to go off much to the delight of the culprit.

Dad bought an old '50 Chevy coupe when I was in high school. I considered that "my car"

My old '50 Chevy changed drastically after I left home. Delano bought it from Dad and put a 322 Buick engine in it, an Olds transmission and a newer Chevy rear end. That dead-head looking thing would fly.

One day, shortly after Delano finished working on it, he and a friend were coming back from Greenfield when Dr. Barr, who was the family doctor in Fontanelle, passed him up in his new Chrysler New Yorker. Delano asked his friend, "Do you want to have some fun," and of course the answer was yes. They went around Dr Barr like he was sitting still. Dr. Barr chased them all the way back to the D-X to ask, "What in the hell kind of car is that?"

Delano and Cal became pretty good buddies so it was not unusual to find Cal "shooting the breeze" at the D-X. Evenings when the Station was not busy would find them leaned back in their chairs in the shop area. One day while Cal and Delano were talking Delano brought out a rifle and asked Cal if he thought he could shoot out the light on the water tower. Oh my, that was just down Cal's alley. I can just see him now with a smile on his face and rubbing his hand across his mouth while the wheels turned in his head. "Are you serious?" he asked hoping Delano was. He probably took the 30-30 in his hands, making sure there were no pedestrians or cars around to witness his action, aimed, shot and missed. Pching. The bullet bounced off the tower and Delano took his turn. And so the late evening entertainment went on until the light no longer shone in the night. In a few days the town workers crawled all the way up the ladder on the side of the tower to put a new light in and on another quiet evening the mischievous man and prodigy boy were delighted to be back to their target practice.

CHAPTER TWENTY

I did enjoy the time Dad and I had together when traveling. Road trips with Dad were pleasant and often produced a story or interesting details from his past. His compassions for animals or less fortunate people were obvious when he talked about finding a home for a piglet wandering on the side of the road or buying a meal for a penniless hitchhiker. Our trip to Winterset yielded a story about a young lady in search of her lost love.

"It was right along in here," he began, "I was coming home from work one evening when I saw a young girl on the road. She was wet from her knees down. It was a hell of a cold day for anyone to be out in the weather, let alone someone with soaked clothing. I wanted to help her but thought it would be safer if I had someone else along when I picked her up so I drove the mile or so back to the quarry to ask Jack Brown to follow me. There is always the possibility that a situation is not as simple as it looks."

Jack followed Dad to the place where he saw the girl. She was just starting to climb over a fence when they arrived. Dad asked her if she needed a ride and the girl gratefully climbed into his red company pickup. She was cold and shivering. As they traveled from the isolated area she began to tell him her story.

"Where were you going?" Dad began the conversation.

"I saw a cabin in the field back there. I was trying to get there. I thought I could spend the night," she told him.

"You would freeze to death before morning if you slept there," he told her. "Why are you out here all alone in this cold weather?"

Exhausted and chilled the broken-hearted girl began to sob, "I'm going to California. My boyfriend moved there and I want to be where he is." Poor child was from somewhere near Ohio and had traveled, most likely hitch-hiked, from there to Winterset where her ride let her off. She had walked to this uninhabited stretch of road without any more ride offers.

"Where in California does he live?" Dad asked.

"I don't know his address," she confessed.

"Don't you think you should go back to your folks?" He asked. "California is a long way to go."

She spun a sad tale about not having a real home and how she had lived with relatives and often moved from one home to another.

Dad took her on into Greenfield to the hotel. With a ten dollar bill he reserved a room for her and gave her the remaining three or four dollars to get something to eat. Dad saw her eying a chocolate bar display on the counter. "Would you like to have that candy bar," he asked.

She nodded. "Yes I would." He gave her the bar and the money and continued on to his warm home where supper was waiting.

A few days later the hotel clerk saw Dad and told him how glad he was Dad brought her there. "I wondered what happened to her," Dad asked hoping the clerk knew.

"One of the regular customers took an interest in her. He talked her into going back to her home," the clerk told him. Dad was relieved that others had taken an interest in her and helped her make a better choice. At least she would be in familiar surroundings with people she knew.

CHAPTER TWENTY-ONE

One morning at breakfast an incriminating conversation started, "I found my 8th grade graduation certificate was lying on top of some papers. Do you know how it got there?" Dad asked.

No. Where was it supposed to be?" I asked hoping to make sense of what was starting. "Were you in the filing cabinet?"

His memory was hazy. He seemed to only have bits and pieces of information that did not make sense. "No, gawd damn it! That's why I'm asking you. If I had been there I would know it," he stormed.

Other strange things happened that night such as a reorganization of the recycle sacks. He had put three cup hooks on the door to the basement and hung plastic shopping bags on each one: one for plastics, one for cans, and one for clear glass. There was plastic stuffed in the tin cans and a light bulb in with the glass. "Maybe you were sleepwalking," I suggested.

"You just think I'm crazy," he puffed up trying to protect his pride and make me back down.

"You don't have to be crazy to walk in your sleep." I said and tried to reason with him but that rationale was wasted on him and only made him angrier.

Later that day I saw the certificate lying on top of the filing cabinet. There was only one way it could have gotten there but he wasn't admitting it.

Eventually he began talking about looking for the title to the house which I knew was kept in the same general vicinity of the certificate. The man trusted no one and I was on the top of his list of people to distrust. It was then I realized he had been looking for the title to the house to make sure his potentially wicked daughter was not trying to take over his command.

There was the time I washed the towels and tried so hard to put them right back where I found them. One towel hung on his closet door to use after his bath, two hand towels hung on the top of the shower doors, a set of towels hung on the shower door rack for Irene's use when she visited, and a towel on the sink rack. Oh yes, and one on the back of the commode seat. This last towel was there so when he got ready to sit down to put his shoes and socks on, he could pull the towel forward covering the lid. He always put his shoes and socks on before his overalls and he didn't like sitting on the cold seat.

After I finished the laundry, he came to the stairs and demanded to know where his towel was. "What towel?" I asked innocently.

"The towel I use to wipe the shower down. The one that hangs on top of the shower doors." he demanded.

"I put them all back where they belong."

His fury was totally inappropriate for the "offense" I had committed. "Dad, Can we argue about something important? It is here somewhere. It will turn up," I argued.

He raged, "This IS important. Those are MY towels." He eventually found the hand towel he thought was missing but there was no apology.

Occasionally I had control of my emotions enough to see the humor of a situation. That was the case with the vacuum cleaner episode.

I got my vacuum out so I could do a thorough cleaning in the living room. I told Dad I wanted to use my Rainbow vacuum with the beater bar, which I thought would clean the carpet better. Of course he thought his vacuum would do just fine. The first thing that happened was my beater bar froze up and I had to work on it. I sat down on the floor with a screw driver and removed the bottom plate on the beater bar and began inspecting to find the problem. Just as I was getting a handle on what to do when his comment was – "I could have the carpet cleaned by the time you get yours running." Just what I had expected him to say.

The next comment was, "How can you tell how much dirt you have gotten?" His electric broom had a clear plastic container that collected dirt. My vacuum had a water pan. So when I got through vacuuming, I dumped the water pan in a plastic bag and poked a hole in it so the water drained off the dirt so that we could compare his pile of dirt to mine. Robert asked me who won and I told him it depended on who you asked.

The day after this incident Dad couldn't get his TV to work and wanted to know if I knew what was wrong with it. I reminded him we had cleaned the living room the day before and maybe something was disturbed. "Well, you didn't clean behind the TV, did you," he demanded. "That dirt was there a long time and it didn't bother anything. Don't be messing around behind my TV." The plug had come out of the wall. I grinned at him, plugged it in and went back upstairs.

The saga of the vacuum cleaner continued as I wrote to a friend in an email:

"Sorry to hear your mom is not doing well. Unfortunately it is something all of us have to go through if we outlive them and I am not sure I will outlive my 94 year old dad. Robert asked me what I was doing this morning and I told him I was just getting Dad riled a bit to keep him going and warmed up for the day. What did I do you ask?? I thought you never would. Well it is the vacuum cleaner again. We have three electric brooms and a shop vacuum all in one room. #1 broom is his favorite but I vacuumed under his bed and it hasn't worked since. He used it just after that and he thinks he broke it. You don't think I am going to try to convince him otherwise do you? Not me, honey! I did mention it, but he was sure he had caused the damage and it was his fault. Since I don't argue with him (he's always right—according to him) I let him take the responsibility.

The #2 broom Robert bought at an auction, probably for a dollar or two. It works fine but isn't as powerful as #1 and there is no off/on switch. You just have to plug it in. That wasn't good enough so Dad bought a new broom which is #3. Now I won't use #3 because I am afraid it will quit working.

When one of the brooms is used, he uses the shop vacuum to clean the dirt collected out of the bag-less brooms. Then he has to clean the shop vacuum out.

This morning I decided to clean the hall way which is only about 6 feet square. The brooms do not clean the corners so I was taking the shop vacuum to the hall to clean and was pulling it by the hose. Of course, I didn't know the hose pulled out easily and it came out. That aggravated Dad because I should have known better. He grabbed it up by the handle and toted it to the hall for me fussing all the way. I finally am becoming accustomed to the fussing and attitudes. I sat down on the floor and cleaned all around the outside edges of the hall carpet with very little static from Dad. I couldn't hear him over the noise of the vacuum anyway, so it was easy to ignore him. When I finished the edges, I quickly went over the middle with the same attachment. You can be sure I got a comment about that. Oh well.

Broken-down #1 still sits in the room with the #2, #3 and the shop vacuum because some day he may find an old vacuum like it with an impeller in good condition to replace the broken one. Oh yes, there is another old vacuum in the hall closet, one or two in the attic and one in the coat closet, I brought my Rainbow and have a spare Rainbow in the storage building up town. We need to go into business selling the things. I don't think antique vacuums are worth much though."

CHAPTER TWENTY-TWO

After each of our frequent conflicts Dad most likely could be found at his classmate's home. Mildred is an amazing little woman. In her younger days she worked as a school teacher and has a remarkable memory. It was a delight to sit and talk with her and learn many things she could remember about people, places or events. She is also an organized person who was treasurer of her church for the past 50 years and managed a farm business.

Mildred has more knowledge about the town and the people in it than anyone else around. I bet she even takes pride in the fact that she knows more about everyone than they know about themselves. Dad used to say, "I don't know how she does it. If I can't remember something or somebody's name or who they were married to or to whom they were related, I can ask Mildred and she will know." It was fun to visit with her, but I wondered what she knew about me since she hinted she knew more than I thought she did. Dad's confidant, I should have known. "Get a grip," I told myself. It is not important. After all, everybody talks.

She and Dad are buddies. I think it is so amazing they have been friends for so many years. They are a wonderful example of "friends for life".

Dad would tell me he was going for a drive and he soon could be found at Mildred's. No doubt he went there to cuss and discuss how I was intruding into his world and trying to undermine his entire existence. It was also Mildred's delight to unburden herself to Dad about her woes with her children. Maybe it would be interesting to be a "fly-on-the-wall" and hear some of their conversations, but then my ears probably would be severely charred.

I often wondered if Mildred got him riled by telling him his daughter would do the same thing to him that her children were doing to her or, if on some days, it was the other way around. She was a frail woman exactly nine months younger than Dad and, of course, her children only did what they felt was best for her.

At supper I often heard how Mildred's children were "mean" to her, wanting to move her into an apartment five miles away from the town she had lived in all her life. I did sympathize with her. Dad said, "If she wants to die in that house, they should just leave her alone." I guess Dad just wanted to die in his house too, but I didn't leave him alone either.

CHAPTER TWENTY-THREE

Robert had heard Dad's unreasonable "debates" about things being stolen whenever he misplaced something. The night before we were to leave for a short visit in Arkansas he witnessed one of the rages directed at me.

We were all packed and ready to leave the following morning. We had gone to bed early when Dad stormed up the stairs clad in his undershirt and shorts. "Daughter, you could have at least left me one damned roll of toilet paper!" He accused.

Bewildered, Robert and I both sat up in bed to find out what he was talking about. Robert found his voice first. "What are you talking about, Ivan," he asked in his always controlled voice.

"There isn't even one roll of paper in the bathroom."

"Yes, there is, Ivan. It's right there between the sink and the tub," Robert assured him.

Dad respected Robert too much to suspect him of anything. But me – I was the bandit. "Well,

I'll go back down and look again."   In a few minutes he was back at the bottom of the stairs apologizing.

That last attack just made me more anxious to go back to Arkansas and stay as long as I could.   I returned to Arkansas wondering if Dad would miss us or if he would be glad we were gone.

CHAPTER TWENTY-FOUR

So far it seemed as if circumstances planned our every move. Deborah would be starting high school, which made it a good time to change schools. We put the house in Arkansas up for sale and we had a buyer in less than two weeks. With a depressed housing market and foreclosures at an all-time high we just couldn't consider not selling, especially at the price we were asking and with a buyer willing to pay. Since we had a buyer for the house there was a lot of business that needed to be taken care of and if it took all summer, it would be okay with me. After only a few weeks with Dad, I wasn't sure I could tolerate living with him until Robert retired.

What a whirlwind that week was! I helped finish packing, cleaning out the house, and getting ready to sell anything we could not use in Iowa. We had yard sales to get rid of everything that wasn't absolutely necessary and did not have significant sentimental value. I had a buyer for the bed on the first day of the yard sale so Robert set the camper up for us to sleep in.

Dad's calendar was marked for my expected return but only three days after my arrival in Arkansas, he called saying he was not feeling well and wanted to know when I would be returning. This was really putting a monkey wrench in my plans. Was he really feeling bad or was this just another attempt to control?

Although I had originally said I would be gone 10 days to two weeks, I really wanted to spend even more time in Arkansas. I called my sister-in-law, Marsha, to ask what her assessment was of his health. She assured me he did not seem to be any different than usual and would keep a check on him. I still felt uneasy about leaving him. It was unusual for him to admit he needed me. I decided I could accomplish most of what needed to be done in one week and told him I would return as soon as I could. He called often wanting to know when I was coming. Either his memory was not retaining the information or he was prodding me to return. I thought this could be a devious tactic but in retrospect I believe he had been alone for so many years that our presence and help was more welcome and needed than he would admit—if he could only accept the help without dictating and/or criticizing my every move.

CHAPTER TWENTY-FIVE

When I returned to Iowa there were so many appointments to keep up with. Dad was already going to therapy for a shoulder injury. I made an appointment with his family doctor. I noticed Dad was retaining quite a bit of fluid. Although most noticeable on his feet and ankles, his shirts were gaping slightly in the front.

At the first appointment I asked the doctor if he thought Dad might have congestive heart failure. He checked the medical record and said Dad had not been checked for heart problems in a long time, other than pacemaker checks. He scheduled Dad to return to the heart clinic for testing and blood work and prescribed medication for fluid retention. Every day he returned to the hospital for a weight check. It was hard to believe! Within three days he went from buttons gaping open to having three or four inches of extra room in his shirt. It was such a relief to see his progress. He was feeling better, sleeping better, and breathing better. He lost eleven pounds in one week!

A few days later the doctor called and asked us to come to the office to get the results of the testing. Dad's kidney function was holding ok but the heart test showed his heart was only functioning at seventeen per cent. Fifty-five percent is considered normal. The doctor was amazed he could continue to do all he did with such poor heart function. He was placed on two more meds and he began to improve significantly.

Before the medication he could not eat a meal without falling asleep at the table and he could not go to a dance without dozing off in his chair.

Dad fussed about having to take medicine. He thought his heart was working ok. "If my heart was not doing its job, I would know it. I don't know why they want my heart to work harder," he complained. "Why do I need these pills?" "How do you know I need these pills?" "How does the doctor know what I need?" "He doesn't know what my heart feels like." "How do these pills know where to go and what to do?" "Maybe they are counteracting each other."

I really wanted him to understand his heart as well as he understood engines. Fixing an engine, adding on to our house, working with any type of tool, solving almost any visible problem was not a mystery to him. Without any reasonable explanation, he was able to direct Schildberg Construction to a location he thought was a good place to mine for more gravel.

He was right. That gravel pit has produced for over 50 years and is still operating. Maybe that was why he thought he should know what his body needed.

I began asking him questions about how a motor runs, about compression, etc. Finally I asked him, "Isn't that a little like the way your heart works?" He gave it a little thought and decided there might be some similarities. At least it gave him something to think about.

As he continued to take the meds, I noticed a great improvement in his stamina, but not in his attitude. He constantly complained he didn't want to take the pills. It became a daily event – I tried to gently reason with him to help him understand. He got angry and the fight was on. He didn't want to understand. He had his mind set in a certain direction and reason had nothing to do with it.

Again I tired of the constant bickering he enjoyed. "I am not arguing with you again about these pills. Either you take them or you don't. I will fix your weekly pill box and put it on the table but I will not have this conversation with you again!" I exclaimed.

At last I had put my foot down. He was a little shocked, I suppose, that his little girl had gotten so bold. At last we had it out over the yelling and arguing. The next morning it started again. "I told you yesterday I can't handle this constant bickering and I meant it! I am out of here." He started to grab my arm. "Don't grab me," I glared at him for the first time in my life.

By this time we were standing nose to nose. "I'm sorry, okay?" He was nearly shouting but he finally believed me. I hugged his rigid frame and the issue was over.

Amazingly it worked. The pills were off limits to discussions. Occasionally I heard him almost start in on the subject, but he caught himself and stopped midsentence.

Over time I became confident he had recovered enough strength to be able to drive without falling asleep at the wheel. He began going to the places he was familiar with. When I drove for him, he gave me exact and specific directions. "There is a stop light ahead, you need to slow down," or "Turn into the right lane and then move over to the left." Every detail was engraved into his mind and I knew he would go over each one as he drove alone.

CHAPTER TWENTY-SIX

Dad continued to attend dances where he got the best exercise for his condition. I danced very little but enjoyed the music and watched how every couple danced. The Wednesday night dance was at the Chicken Inn. We had our "group" that always sat together. Bud and Ruth always arrived first to save a table for the rest of us.

Dad and I had to leave the house by 3:30, drive 30 miles to Creston so he would have plenty of time to eat his favorite meal. We would always go to the Hy-Vee grocery deli. His meal never changed. It consisted of a large fried chicken thigh, mashed potatoes with white gravy and broccoli salad. After eating we would continue on to the 6:00 dance. He thought he had to be there by 5:00 to be sure we had our usual seats. Bud and Ruth were always first to arrive at our table. After our arrival Doris and Larry and their friend Colleen joined us. Everyone brought snacks to contribute to their group's table. The band took a 30 minute break at 7:30 and each table used the time to visit and eat.

Although the place was no longer called The Chicken Inn, anyone knew where you were going if you mentioned it by its former name. It once was a very popular place for the younger crowds to eat and dance. Now it stands, very much as it was 50 years ago, antiquated and unimproved, hosting dances weekly for seniors.

It was seldom you saw a non-retired couple at the dances. I knew everyone there by sight, how they danced and who they danced with. This particular dance had walk-on musicians. Sometimes there were as many as 20 playing at one time. The musicians were mostly guitar players. The owner's wife was an excellent keyboardist. Occasionally a harmonica, banjo, tambourine, or spoons joined the group, but the biggest treat for my Dad was when a little brass was added to the music.

As the patrons came in, they signed a sheet if they wanted a turn to sing with the band. Most singers were very good but there was the occasional singer with minimal talent. That wasn't important. They were there for the exercise, interaction and enjoyment of being with others of similar interests. My favorite performers were the lady who could yodel and a tenor who loved to sing "Rambling Rose".

On the first and third Saturdays we went to the American Legion in Corning. Again Ruth and Bud were there first. They were such a sweet couple.

Both had lost their first spouse and met at a dance. Bud is a very tall man, over six feet, who has difficulty walking. Dad would probably call him a "best friend". Ruth is a tiny woman, only about five feet tall. She could be considered the "hostess" of our group, very congenial and pleasant. Bud danced very little but Ruth danced as many times as she could which was quite a lot. When *"Waltz Across Texas"* is played, Bud always dances with Ruth.

Some nights Dad danced a lot, and other nights the crowd was slightly different and he did not dance nearly so much. I danced with him a few times when I knew he was not getting as many invitations to dance as he liked. The only problem I had was that I did not have the stamina or leg strength to dance as much as he did. Almost everyone there could dance the entire 3 hours with very little rest. If I got three dances in, I was doing well.

The big treat at Corning is the pot luck supper served at 7:30. Dad loves to eat and he doesn't want to miss out on a meal—especially if it only costs $3.00. He always takes a box of Honey Buns. That is okay for a widower to bring, but once I started going to the dance with him, we needed to provide more appropriately. He has a hard time understanding Why I want to buy something different or cook something to take. He continues to take the Honey Buns and complains nobody eats them.

At this dance spot I began to realize how much These people love to dance. There are people who come in with walkers, canes and oxygen. The man with oxygen pulls off his nasal cannula and hits the dance floor. He might not dance long, but he gets out there. Another puts his cane down, just barely shuffles to the floor, and then performs an impressive two-step right along with everyone else. There are usually three people in their nineties at every dance.

The nicest place to dance is at the Raccoon Ridge. It is located about six miles north of Stuart. Most of that mileage is down a crooked, narrow, hilly, gravel road. The music hall is very nice even though it sets in the middle of a corn field.

Linda and Gary Thompson created their "Field of Dreams" not only because of their love of music, but also because they felt they were blessed financially and wanted to share their abundance with others. The movie statement, "If you build it, people will come" is as true for their music hall as it was for the baseball field in the movie.

One man came in on two canes and Ruth said, "I bet he doesn't dance, just enjoys the music." After what I saw at other places, I was not at all surprised to see him on the floor. Sure enough, he danced. At first he just stood at the corner of the dance floor with his partner and kind of rocked back and forth. He had the most pleasant smile on his face. Eventually he did venture toward the center of the dance floor. One gentleman who looked older than my Dad and skinny as a scare crow was once a dance instructor. His dance style was smooth and impressive. Another couple danced the jitter bug like they were still in high school. They are a few years older than me but they can do old time rock and roll faster and better than anyone else. This was where I first met the pretty blonde who liked to polka with Dad. She was a knockout, always neatly groomed, well-portioned and dressed to enhance her figure. Her partner was not able to do the polka with her due to back problems so "the blonde", as Dad called her, darted over to our table as soon as she heard polka music start.

The Eagles has been another popular spot for dancers over the past 50 years or more. Unlike the Chicken Inn, it has recently modernized and is well kept. It is versatile with an ample dance floor separated from a spacious bar. A nice dining area is also available as are newly remodeled restrooms. The atmosphere there is more like I am used to. Gary and Linda from Raccoon Ridge were the musicians on the night we were there.

Deborah and her friend, Candys, wanted to go with us. Since I had not been there before, I asked Dad if it was ok for them to go with us and he said it was. They had a great time. I gave each of them

$5.00 and told them to make it last. There is a short non-alcoholic bar on the dance floor level where they sat and ate popcorn and drank sodas. Later I noticed they were not visible so I began searching for them. The curious teens had explored the club and found their way to the wet bar and were playing pool. Since there were only a couple people there, the atmosphere was less like a bar and more like a game room to them and the waitress seemed to enjoy having them there. After assessing their surrounding, I thought it seemed innocent enough and let them continue to enjoy the free game.

To my delight, Aunt Susie her husband, Marlin, arrived at the dance. That made the evening perfect!

CHAPTER TWENTY-SEVEN

Although each aunt is a special person, Susie is my favorite. There is so much to tell about her I don't know where to begin. I guess her 14th birthday is a good place to start. That was the day I was born, back in the days when the doctors still made house calls and babies could be delivered at home. She lived about half a mile from my home and came to the house riding her bicycle with a blanket neatly placed in the basket on the front. She was planning to take me home in the basket. I was her birthday present! Mom didn't think that was a good idea.

After Susie graduated from high school, the same school that both Dad and I graduated from, she continued her education by attending a beauty school in Des Moines. She and her oldest sister, Izola, (my Mom was the middle sister) lived in an apartment together. Nearly every summer I got to go stay with one or both of them. On my first visit, Susie took me to work with her. Since little kids sometimes get in the way or bored, Susie decided to let me go to the movies by myself. She walked me the half block to the theater, paid my admission and asked the usher in the theater to keep an eye on me. I arrived back at the beauty school only a few minutes after I was left at the theater. "Why did you come back so soon," Susie asked me.

"The movie was over," I announced thinking I knew what I was talking about. I only watched the cartoon. That was probably my first visit to the theater and I didn't know there was always a cartoon before the movie started. Susie just chuckled and decided not to take me back to watch the main attraction. I was perfectly happy to stay at the shop and play with the tools of her trade.

After beauty school Susie married Dale, a handsome man with a great smile and dark, curly hair, and moved to a farm. It was even more fun to stay with Aunt Susie and Uncle Dale. I went to the hen house three or four times a day to check for eggs. I loved to climb the hay bales in the barn and roam around the pastures. I couldn't get lost. All I had to do was follow one of the cow trails and I was back at the house in no time. I loved the willow tree in the back yard with the thin branches that touched the ground. It was like a little hideout or play house.

One ill-fated day my uncle and I were playing around the barn yard. I got a bucket of water and chased him pretending I was going to throw it on him. At last he tired of the game and stopped in front of me. He waited a minute to give me an opportunity to douse him, but I was so excited I just stood there with the bucket and giggled. That scoundrel took my bucket and poured the water on me! I responded like a wet hen. After all, I wasn't really going to get him wet. I was so upset I sat in the hen house all afternoon pouting and drying my socks.

I always had fun at Aunt Susie's whether it was trying to mow her yard, or planning a special dinner for Uncle Dale, digging around in her attic, or trying to put up Christmas decorations in July. She was so patient.

Uncle Dale liked to take me to town with him. One day he was taking his baby piglets to market. He picked them up by their little curly tails and tossed them in the trunk of his car. On another trip he took his car to be worked on. I decided to stay in the car while it was hoisted up in the air. I was easily entertained and that day I found a travel alarm clock to play with. When the alarm sounded, the mechanic could not imagine where the sound was coming from. Uncle Dale never tired of telling the story about the confused mechanic. As a matter of fact, he loved to tease me about a number of things that happened when I visited their farm.

CHAPTER TWENTY-EIGHT

Dad's outburst that shook me the most came about two months after we returned from Arkansas. Although much improved, Dad still had not adjusted to my presence in his domain and his health improvements did not improve his disposition. This final extreme outburst probably came after another disturbing conversation with Mildred. I doubt seriously he could tell anyone specifically why he was angry. He stood at the base of the stairs and shouted, "You come down here." I calmly but hesitantly came down the stairs and faced him one step above his already short stature, Deborah was perched on the top stair looking on. She was wide-eyed and wondering what was going to happen.

He stood there with his frail chest pushed out as he might have done in his younger days when he faced some younger person or smaller person or maybe one of those cocky younger guys wearing Bermuda shorts that he worked with at Schildbergs. They were just kids fresh out of high school who worked on the crushing crew. He knew he could intimidate them. And now it was my turn to face him. "Go ahead, touch me, just touch me," he dared. Carefully assessing the situation and knowing I had all the advantages of being younger, just a little more agile, and probably able to block him if he actually decided to throw a punch, I slowly and gently touched him on the shoulder. "Well it had better be easy," he said in a slightly less pushy voice knowing now I had called his bluff and he had lost.

I may have called his bluff, but he had shaken my nerves to the point I knew I was in trouble. Later that day I was still upset over the incident. I fiercely attacked Dad verbally. "I don't think what you did was funny at all. I can't take this any more. You have two weeks. If you continue to throw fits, I am moving out."

Two days later, still exhausted and trembling, I called Robert. "Are you getting your replacement trained," I asked with feigned calmness.

"He's doing all right," Robert replied thinking I was just chatting but my next sentence gave me away.

"Do you think you could come to Iowa sooner than you had planned – like now?" I asked still trying to control my tone.

He knew by the tremble in my voice it was urgent. Robert did not waste any time. He left

Arkansas just after lunch that day and arrived the following afternoon. It was just what I needed.

Dad did not know Robert was coming. I kept it a secret. When Robert arrived Dad reacted a little like he had been caught with his hand in the cookie jar. He knew Robert had arrived early for a reason but nothing was ever said about what the reason was. Robert stayed about three weeks. It was enough time to give me rest and calm Dad down. We planned more frequent visits to help keep the stress level as low as possible.

CHAPTER TWENTY-NINE

Things always went much better when Robert was with us. He fixed breakfast every morning and let me get the rest Dad did not allow me when I needed it so much. Although situations were much better controlled, they were not perfect and having Robert there could always make a bad situation go away with much less friction — like the toothbrush episode.

"Did you get in the medicine cabinet last night," Dad asked and I knew trouble was brewing.

"I don't ever bother anything in your cabinet," I told him honestly.

"My toothbrush is not in the same place I put it. I thought maybe you or Deb used it by mistake." He was trying gently to lay blame on Deb. He blamed Deb for almost everything that wasn't the way he thought he had left it from the treadmill not being turned off to cutting the toe out of his socks.

"No, Dad, Deb has her own toothbrush and so do I."

On and on the disturbing debate on the toothbrush continued.

On another day I heard, "My toothbrush is turned around backwards. Come here and see." Like that was going to prove anything.

A few days later he noticed the toothbrush bristles were flattened and again I was summoned to see. "Look Dad," I said as I turned the toothbrush around in the holder to show him what affect that position might make on the bristles. Another tirade began.

"Do you think I am crazy? I would know if I had done that. Someone was in here besides me," he stormed.

The only way I knew to diffuse the situation was to just be quiet or to agree with him.

The night before Deb had spent the night with Candys. "Deb wasn't here last night," Robert told him, "and I know I didn't do it."

He finally conceded probably because Robert said it. "I guess I am crazy," he said.

"No, you are not crazy. We all do things a little differently from time to time and don't remember. You are ok," I assured him.

Why did I do that? I would have felt better if I had jumped on the table and screamed, "Yes you are nuts!"

Near the end of this visit Robert and I attended a workshop on caregivers that was very helpful in understanding the dementia-type behavior Dad was occasionally exhibiting. Although I thought this might be the problem, I did not understand how his mind was working. I didn't understand that his security came from knowing exactly where everything was. His mind had sort of a photograph of what was normal and any little thing out of place caused him to feel unbalanced and confused.

Now I had more insight. I understood his need to keep things in specific places and it was much easier to deal with the things he said and overlook things he did. When he told me I was fat, I agreed. If he thought we had meddled in his things, we decided it was probably that "other man" that we knew very well (Dad's humorous way of referring to himself) who had been there. If he tried to start an argument or intentionally aggravate me, I ignored him.

After Robert's visit I was rested and able to handle life in my Father's house again. Dad's total demeanor was mellowed. Life was not perfect, but living was within reasonable boundaries.

CHAPTER THIRTY

The epic winter I witnessed was enchanting – at least at first. It became a fairyland of snow and ice. I doubt that anyone else enjoyed it as much as I did. The first snow came on October first. With the ground still warm it was much too early for snow and our four inches of fluffy white flakes only lasted a few days. We did not see any more snow until December when our state was inundated with a blizzard along with several bouts of snow. The first snow brought us about six to eight inches and then the blizzard brought enough more snow to add up to more than fifteen inches on the ground.

I hinted to Dad early on in the year I needed some space to park my car during the winter months, but my appeal fell on deaf ears.

Dad has plenty of places to park vehicles out of the weather, but they are all full. The garage attached to the house shelters his Ford tractor with attached snow plow ready to attack the residue of each snow fall. The basement garage is a perfect place for his equipment during the winter months.

Dad just goes down the stairs to the basement garage, opens the door and drives into the snow without going outside—a convenience a man his age deserves. But it really isn't quite that simple. All of Dad's equipment is incredibly outdated and requires frequent maintenance. Once the repairs are completed it is easy to get to the task at hand.

It is amazing that Dad can manipulate so many vehicles to fit inside his double garage/workshop. This building houses not two but four vehicles – a green, 1927 Model T he restored himself (including sewing the upholstery), a seldom-to-never driven ominous old three-quarter ton, diesel pickup with camper shell, a 1989 Buick Regal he loves, and a 2004 Buick LaSabre he doesn't love.

Dad's '89 Regal could do no wrong. If it missed or stalled, it could be fixed. If he drove the LeSabre there was constant chatter on how it didn't hold the road like his Regal. "I just don't like this car," he told me every time he drove it. "I don't think it likes me either."

The camper shed was vacated last summer when Dad decided to send the camper to Arkansas with us. The camper had set unused for more than ten years when he first offered it to us, but then changed his mind saying, "It is good company". Last year he finally released his camper into our custody and the shed was reoccupied with Dad's covered boat and three riding lawn mowers – the old John Deere he loved, the new Cub Cadet he didn't love, and my husband's mower with the triple-bagger something-or-other on it.

His antique John Deere mower receives constant attention to repair its worn, obsolete parts. In summer he spent days working on it so he could use it and ignored the pristine Cub Cadet mower sitting patiently in the shed waiting its turn. It had to wait until my husband was there before it would get a chance to perform. Dad's Ford tractor was also in the shed during the summer months but during the winter months it needed to be more accessible for snow removal.

I calmly accepted the chilling fact my vehicle would remain in the elements. As it turned out, it deserved to be outside since it was like a whale in the desert when it came to snow and ice. The Yukon I loved was a tad disgusting in winter and may not have climbed the sloped driveway to the road even if it had been sheltered.

The snow plows managed to bury my Yukon on one side and a snow drift on the other side was at least 3 feet high. I viewed my Yukon's dilemma in the snow with little concern. After living in the south for decades, I had forgotten what it was like when winters lasted for months. I thought that the snow would probably melt down in a few days. I scooped off the porch and managed to make a trail to the mound of snow left by the city's snow plow. It was enough for a dog run and to help me get to my van. When I got to my van it started but I quickly discovered it was not going to be able to climb over the mounds of snow.

Dad was busy solving his own predicament. Driving was the one thing he loved to do. It was what gave him something to do when he became bored sitting in the house. I have never counted the number of times he left the house to go for a drive but it would not surprise me if it numbered around six or more times a day. At this moment his car was inaccessible and that was unacceptable.

First he called the city office to ask them to bring their equipment to clear the right-of-way on the far side of the two-car garage. He then had much less snow to move with his old Ford tractor with the twenty year-old battery. Several homes in Fontanelle depended on Wayne to bring his huge, yellow snow plow/front-end loader to keep their drives clear in winter but Dad was not one of them. This was one time Dad needed more help than usual. He called Wayne to clear the snow in front of the double garage and the upper part of the driveway. Soon Dad was in the basement garage where his tractor was stored. I watched him start his tractor. I couldn't believe a man who was so particular in everything he did used a pair of pliers with insulated handles to touch a couple of points causing sparks to fly, but he did and the engine began putt-putt-putting away. I opened the garage door for him and he was off. Dad removed enough snow from the lower half of the drive to connect with the right-of-way cleared by the city. He could now reach his car and go whenever he was in the mood.

Now I wondered about my van. I suspected I might have to shovel the snow away from it eventually but I was not going to do it right away. The next day we heard equipment running in our front yard. We looked out the windows and discovered someone using a snow blower to help clear out our walkway. Wow! What a nice person! He even began to work on clearing some of the snow piles beside my van. I dressed in my warmest clothes and went outside to see who it was and if I could get my van out now. I discovered it was John, our neighbor, for whom Dad had cleared snow in years past and now the neighbor was returning the favor. We were all very grateful – but no one appreciated it more than I!

I started my van and sat there letting it warm up. I moved it back and forth a little to help get more room for John to remove snow. As I sat there another man came zooming around the corner in a bobcat and took a few quick, well-orchestrated runs at removing the snow in front of my van making a huge pile of snow in the center of the yard. He drove in, helped without being asked and disappeared just as quickly as he came without saying a word. It was quite a sight to see so many activities taking place at one time and such a relief when my van was free at last.

My Deborah had seen so little snow in her lifetime that this commotion was invigorating to her. She climbed the mounds of snow and slipped down and ran through the snow blower's spray in a way that reminded me of summer, swim suits and water sprinklers. When she climbed her first twenty-foot mound of snow she told me she thought it might give away under her feet like new snow and she would be at the bottom unable to get out. Fortunately the snow plow created this hard-packed mound when clearing a parking lot and she was safe.

As the winter continued, we had more snow, freezing rain, and lots of record-setting, sub-zero temperatures. When the roads were cleared and the sun finally came out, the sights were spectacular. The trees glistened with an icy coating on every branch, the power lines looked like silvery threads draped from pole to glistening pole. Chain link fences were a grid of shining ice. Fence posts and wire were as blindingly beautiful the power lines. Every field was white with snow and every corn stalk stub left from harvesting was a gleaming spike.

Just as I thought I had seen the most stunning sites winter could produce, Mother Nature produced a new situation to awe my mind. The winds blew snow banks so high and billowy that snow plows and snow blowers could only cut the lower bluff away from the road. At last the temperatures warmed up enough that the direct heat of the sun and window defroster managed to soften the ice and snow caked on the Yukon. Although finally free of the clumps of ice frozen under the wipers and the dirty snow slush packed on the mud flaps, the van was still encrusted with the salty road residue. The car wash would be closed until the temperatures were above freezing so the van would just have to be dirty until spring.

I awoke the next morning to another dramatic scene – more snow. This time the branches of the trees were heavily coated with feathery flakes—a new wonderland of lacy white exquisiteness. It seemed winter was showing off as if she were a precocious child with a rapt audience. It was nearly as beautiful as the day my mother was buried.

It was just after Christmas, 1987. Mom and Dad decided to bring their camper to Arkansas and park in our yard for a long visit. Eagerly anticipating their arrival in late November, we prepared a camper pad with water, sewer and electricity.

It was so nice to have them there. My husband and I were both working but spent our evenings with them. Mom and I walked together for her heart exercise. When Mom arrived, she told me her doctor had called to tell her the results from her most recent heart checkup. It was not good news. Her heart had enlarged significantly since her last visit. The worst could happen at any time. She told me she did not want any life support measures taken, but I could not accept the thought of Mom dying. "You know, Mom," I said gently, hoping she understood my motives, "We will do everything we can for you."

She was not one to complain. She took aspirin for pain more than she should so she could keep going. Her body was tired and she knew she could not last much longer. I couldn't face that her death was so near.

We spent Christmas day with Mom and Dad and were invited to eat breakfast with them in El Dorado the day after. However we got up late and decided to skip breakfast. We were to eat with the In-laws that day for lunch. Mom and Dad went on to El Dorado without us, ate, walked in the mall and returned to the camper where mom did their laundry and washed and rolled her hair.

On our way back from the family dinner we stopped to visit friends but planned to be home early. While talking with our friends, we got a phone call that Mom had been taken to the hospital and had died. We were told she carried a laundry basket into the camper when Dad heard her let out a big gasp and slide to the floor. Dad was right outside and immediately went in to her, but it was too late. The ambulance was called but there was nothing they could do for her. I hated it so badly. I wasn't there to help Dad with calling the ambulance or to be with Mom. It was an unforeseen event—something a person cannot know about or prepare for ahead of time.

I went to the hospital where I asked if I could see her. They let me into her room in the emergency area. She was lying on the gurney covered with a white sheet. The curlers were still in her hair. I wanted to touch her or kiss her cheek but somehow I felt she was not there at all—her spirit was already with the Lord and this was just a shell of the woman I had loved all my life. Even at age 41 I felt the loneliness of being orphaned and motherless.

Dad hired a suburban to carry her back to Iowa—$1.00 per mile, 713 miles. It was the worst winter Arkansas had in a long time. Even so, the weather cooperated perfectly. A break in the weather afforded our two-vehicle caravan to travel the cleared roads without difficulty. The northern weather was an exaggerated mirror image of the unusual Southern winter. Almost as soon as our journey was completed the snow storms again assaulted the land. It was nearly a week or maybe more before the funeral services could be held.

I learned an important detail about my mother which made all the difference in my attitude toward the devastating loss I had just suffered. I did not know until Dad mentioned it sometime before the funeral—Mom loved winter. It snowed a lot that year and fresh snow covered the ground the morning of the service. The tree limbs wore a luxurious coat of ice. That morning the sun came out and, even though the temperatures were still very cold, silvery slivers of ice began falling from the branches into the deep, white, unscathed snow. I looked out the kitchen window to the most breath-taking sight I had ever seen and knew it was just for my mother—the most perfect scene nature could create for her. In clouds of untouched snow were the pieces of ice that had fallen from the trees. With the sun shining as brightly as I have ever seen it, those pieces of ice sparkled in the snow like thousands of diamonds and the trees glistened with the ice still remaining on their branches.

At the cemetery it was cold and the wind was blowing but the beauty was comfort. It was a day created for her. My Mother left us in the midst of winter storms and now, 22 years later, my first winter in Iowa was nearly identical.

As winter wore on, the beauty could last no longer. The trees' branches were so heavily laden with ice they sagged to the ground and the picturesque view was now eerily sad. The sky and the ground melded together in a grey mass. The sun seldom broke through the overcast sky. Cracking and breaking sounds of branches could be heard in the house. We fell quiet and listened a few seconds, wondering what the eerie noises were before realizing it was another by-product of winter. The yard was now a jungle of branches. Icy branches that once were glorious now fell on power lines already heavily burdened with their own coating. Utility poles and lines snapped leaving thousands of homes without power for days. Livestock was unable to drink from frozen ponds or troughs. Farmers were busy getting generators to run water lines to the thirsty animals.

And my Dad – what was he doing? He found an opossum beside the road on the other side of town. "Poor little devil," he empathized. He was such a softie where animals were concerned, "He's probably having a hell of a time trying to find something to eat." The following day he collected a piece of orange slice candy and a small slice of fruit cake, "They like sweets," he told me and carried it down to the opossum's site. "I saw a muddy trail in the snow so he must have a hideout nearby," he told me. To Dad's delight the food disappeared at first but in a few days it was left untouched. I thought surely the possum had moved on, but dad did not give up.

The following morning our world was again coated with not only a light snowfall, but also a layer of ice much heavier than the others. Dad was elated to see the tracks of the opossum across the fresh coating. My Yukon looked like it had a form-fitted glass casing. I heard the garage door open and looked out my upstairs window. To my horror I saw my Dad, cane in hand, inching his way toward the shop. In the other hand he had an ice cream bucket full of table scraps.

He stopped midway to empty the bucket for whatever other "poor devils" might visit, usually cats. My first impulse was to knock on the window and tell him to come back to the house, but I feared he would lose his balance and fall, so I just let him go. Finally he reached the shop and I breathed a little easier. I sat back down at the computer, but it wasn't long before I heard the crunching of tires on the frozen driveway. Again I watched, hoping he would not go far. At last he had the car aimed up the driveway and his front-wheel drive LeSabre embarrassed my Yukon. With each try he got up the drive a little further and I was sure the next attempt would get him onto the city street. Frantically I called Robert in Arkansas. "Call my Dad on his cell phone and tell him to get back in the house." Dad and Robert had a much better connection probably because they were likewise endowed. Daughters are females and are ignored where advice is concerned.

"What are you doing today, Ivan," Robert queried him as if I had not called him and he had no idea what the old guy was up to. After several minutes I saw Dad begin to realign the car's direction to get back in the shop and I breathed a little easier.

I watched him inch his way back to the house praying I would not have to call 911 – what good would that do? An emergency vehicle couldn't get here anyway. "I would have been really upset if I had to get dressed and come out there to try to pick you up off the ground," I scolded him.

"I would have been, too," he calmly quipped.

That was not the response I had hoped for. I really wanted him to realize staying in the house during icy conditions was a good idea but changing his lifestyle was not something that would happen any time soon.

"I wanted to go down and see if the opossum ate the food. I decided I probably couldn't go very far on those streets so I just put the car away. They are slicker than snot. I have never seen this much ice."—all that effort just for an opossum. The following day he was able to get his car out and was happy to find his little friend had left new tracks in the snow.

The monster mounds finally began to melt leaving behind the layers of dirt once hidden by each new snow fall. Large pellets of ice fell from the trees. I dreaded driving under them. Every breeze sent a shower of bullets to attack my SUV and I wondered each time if the sun roof would survive. The spring thaw had begun.

CHAPTER THIRTY-ONE

Spring is always refreshing and a welcomed season. This year was no exception. Not only were the ten and twenty-foot mounds of snow melting, flowers beginning to bloom and birds singing but now Robert would be arriving in a few days and I would have a constant advocate between me and Dad. What a relief it would be to have another piece of normal life put into place.

Robert's arrival meant that we were much more crowded than before. Dad and Robert frequently discussed different ways to improve the living arrangements, but the bottom line would always be that Dad was not going to allow any changes.

And then one day FATE, PROVIDENCE, a stroke of good luck, or divine intervention arrived with perfect timing. We had taken every step without knowing what the next step would be and the path seemed to lead straight and clear to a destination we could not have planned any more perfectly.

Robert's internet search for local auctions led him to a real estate foreclosure auction site that had a house for sale two blocks from Dad's house. I had looked at available properties during the past year but none seemed right for us. This house was perfect. Built in 1948, it needed updating and decorating, but it was not more than we could handle. Deb loved her upstairs room at Dad's and this house had two large rooms upstairs that she could have all to herself, a small garage for Robert to store his treasures in and a full basement that I loved.

Dad viewed the house with us. He loved it. Why he ought to buy the house and give us his, was one of his comments, but it was not long before he realized we were seriously considering buying this one. His attitude changed. Dad was not happy that we were looking at another place to live. He told us he didn't think we really wanted to buy a house. He didn't like the small yard where the new house was. His previous blow-in-the-wind comments about helping us buy a house were now totally retracted.

His help or lack of help had never been a consideration in anything I had ever done and so it didn't matter very much what his opinion was on this issue. We would do what was best for our family and continue to be as much help as we could be to Dad.

The day the auction for the house was to end I sat at the computer and anxiously placed our bids. Dad and Robert sat downstairs and watched the progress from Robert's laptop. Dad was stewing. He told Robert he hoped I didn't get the bid. We needed to stay where we were.

There were 17 interested bidders. Most had dropped out before the bids reached $20,000. I placed a bid 26,400 and waited. At last we were notified that we had the winning bid. I knew that we could not have made too big a mistake at that price but I worried anyway. How would we manage the payment, how expensive would the repairs and updates be, etc?

The house turned out to be a true diamond in the rough. It was even better than we had hoped. Part of the original wiring and plumbing had already been updated or replaced. We hired a plumber and an electrician to finish updating. Every room was painted and cleaned and carpets shampooed.

Every day Dad would be there watching us work and fretting. "You won't want my house now." "Things aren't working out the way I planned." "I should have just gone to the nursing home and let you have my house." All were useless comments that not only were too little, too late, but also issues that had already been addressed with no willingness to work with us. We were about to slip out of his spider web and into our own comfort zone and he couldn't stop it. He even got so desperate that he offered to give us $25,000 for the house so that we would have a cushion in the bank. Who knows what strings would have been attached to that. I immediately declined. We used our savings to pay the house off and were dealing with the expenses very well.

It seemed every yard sale or auction or used furniture store had something we needed. Soon the house was attractively furnished. We added a new refrigerator and three new mattresses. Dad held the reins tightly but we still managed to slip out of his control.

CHAPTER THIRTY-TWO

After we were in our own home Dad would eat lunch and supper with us all the while complaining that he liked his kitchen better, he liked his big yard better, he liked his house, etc. But after the first snow and ice came, Dad did not want to get out of his house – even to drive. We then started carrying his meals to his house. Each meal we took was enough for lunch and supper so that we only had to make one trip a day. He was not nearly as adventuresome as he had been the year before. There was no opossum to feed. He didn't want the cat coming to the front door for food. He didn't want to go to dances but he was still ornery enough to try to start arguments. While we were at Dad's house I cleaned up the kitchen a little, gathered his laundry and trash and visited with him while he ate. One day when he finished eating he asked me why he had baking soda. I knew he was up to something. "You probably use it for a sour stomach." I fell into his trap.

"Somebody messed up my baking soda box. Did you do that?" He asked.

"No, Dad. You probably did it."

That was just what he didn't want to hear."I didn't do it." He said with his usual confidence.

"I guess that ghost got in here again." I looked in the drawer and found the box he thought was baking soda. It was corn starch. The top had been ripped and several pieces of scotch tape were attempting to keep it from spilling. I showed it to him and the box of baking soda near it. In order to avoid further confusion, the corn starch went in a bag for me to take home.

I sat down at the table with Dad and Robert and asked Dad if he had given any more thought to going to the nursing home and talked about how nice it would be to have someone doing his laundry, taking care of his pills, cleaning his room and always having people to talk to. "But of course you know you would have to give up your freedom to come and go as you please." I reminded him.

"NO WAY!" He let us know in no uncertain terms. I just laughed a little and changed the subject.

"Do you like wine?" He asked me. Now what is he driving at, I wondered.

"Not really." I responded I thinking he already knew that.

"Well, somebody has been drinking my wine. I just got that bottle yesterday." I opened the refrigerator door and saw a bottle well over half empty. I just let out a belly laugh. That usually throws him off a little and takes the edge off what could be anger.

Robert snickered too. "No wonder you didn't feel good this morning, Ivan. You had a hangover!" Robert loves to josh and can get away with teasing Dad.

"I think Marilyn has been over here." I teased him.

"Do you think so?" He wasn't sure what to think but any time he can find someone else to blame for whatever his woes are, he will take advantage of it. I motioned for Robert to take me home so we could end this nonsense.

"My truck is still running. We better get on back to the house." Robert told him and we left but that was not the end of it.

Now that we lived in our own home, it was a little more difficult for him to irritate me but he didn't give up easily. My phone rang once, "What nursing home were you talking about, the one in Greenfield or the one in Fontanelle?" The phone rang twice, "Should I take the cough syrup or should I cough to get the stuff out of my throat?" The phone rang a third time, "Do you know what happened to that box of stuff that wasn't baking soda?"

He knew he wasn't supposed to call me after 8:00 pm unless it was an emergency so he was making sure he got all his questions asked early. I had imposed the curfew on him a few weeks earlier when he felt quite comfortable calling me at 11:00 pm for some trivial matter, or 3:00 am because he couldn't sleep. Sometimes it would be because that cat wouldn't go away, or maybe it was to find out what time the housekeeper was coming the next day. He took me seriously on the curfew and I was so grateful.

CHAPTER THIRTY-THREE

Dad's annual heart check-up was due in January. I drove him to Des Moines where he was told that he needed a new pacemaker. An appointment was scheduled for the following week. He felt so much better after the surgery that I had mixed emotions about his renewed energy. The good news was the he was able to dance again. The bad news was that he was getting his car out and driving around. As the weeks passed his pacemaker improved his activity level; he seemed to have turned the clock back. The melting snow and warmer weather encouraged his daily jaunts. At first the higher prices for gasoline slowed how far and how often he would venture but when that's all a man has got to do. . .

The pacemaker did not improve mental acuity. It was most evident to me when I changed his sheets. Everything I did for Dad was a turf war. He always fussed that his sheets, and his clothes, didn't need to be washed. When I did get permission to put clean sheets on the bed, he had to be in total charge of every wrinkle, every angle and every detail. Any variance would evoke his anger. If I failed to meet full criteria there was more hollering and swearing than a tribe of Banshee Indians. The tirade was so bad that I nearly lost his housekeeping assistant.

After we moved in our own home, I wanted Dad to have someone to help him keep the house clean. Linda was perfect. She not only had been my friend and neighbor when I was a child but her Dad had worked with my Dad at Schildbergs. Dad was very set against having anyone come in to help him but in a weak moment he commented that he didn't want people to talk about his house being dirty. That opened the door for a housekeeper. I immediately went to the Home Care Office and applied for one.

He didn't like having someone come into his house. If he knew when Linda was coming, he would do all the housekeeping he could before she got there. He is a proud and independent man. Allowing anyone else into his domain was like relinquishing part of his authority. He would only allow her to come once a month but that was a big step.

When Linda arrived for her first cleaning visit Dad was right there in control of every move she made. He put the kitchen chairs on the table he followed her while she vacuumed. He made sure she got into every corner, under every piece of furniture and if he could have found that attachment to vacuum the drapes, he would have had her do that. Before she left she was dripping with sweat. I knew she could not be subjected to that every time so I decided I would try to keep Dad occupied so that she could get some routine mopping and general work done without his interference.

The sheet changing episode occurred during Linda's second cleaning visit. Not only did she witness Dad's temper but when he got loose from me, he again followed Linda's every movement. The following day I got a call from the Home Health Care Agency with concerns about Dad making comments that he didn't need any help. I told them I would talk to Dad.

"Dad, you hurt Linda's feelings." I told him. "She thinks you don't want her to come back."

"Oh, I didn't mean to do that." He was sincere. The "lady's man" side of him came out.

The next sessions went much better. He let Linda clean whatever she wanted to clean and even stayed out of her way – most of the time.

CHAPTER THIRTY-FOUR

Two years after moving to Iowa just about everything got easier. The turf wars became a thing of the past. With the mental changes taking place, changing the sheets is now much easier. He does not recall the exact details that were so important in the past. If I make the bed quickly enough it is done before he has time to remember what he used to fuss about.

Dad wears his overalls and shirts several times before allowing me to wash them. It had been be a fight every time I reminded him that his clothes needed to be washed. Arguing over his clothes is not as important to him. Occasionally he even brings his clothes to me for washing or tells me he is ready to have his sheets changed.

Robert and I notice many signs that his memory is failing. Dad drives his newer car all the time now. When he tries to drive the Regal that he loved so much, it is difficult for him to remember how everything operates. He can drive the LaSabre fine but switching back and forth between vehicles is too difficult.

Dad still lives by himself, fixes his own breakfast and has a housekeeper once a month. We are in our house where I have found rubber bands around packages that have been opened quite practical. There is a towel on the back of the commode seat. It is not there to sit on though. It is there because I have found it is easier to keep that section clean. I just put the towel in the laundry occasionally. When Robert helps me make the bed I try to remember that the wrinkles are not important. Dad has a lot of good ideas but there are things about Dad that I don't want to imitate.

He tries to lure us back to his home by telling us we can do whatever we want the house but when we start to do something it has to either be done his way or not at all. We have assured him that when he is gone we will sell our house, remodel his and live in it – at least in the summer. Winters will find us back in Arkansas where my beloved loves to fish.

At age 96 Dad teeters precariously on the edge of independence. He brings up the nursing home subject often but he is still comfortable in his home. If anyone asks me how he manages to continue to live alone or what accounts for his long life, I would have to say it is the "grit" that exists somewhere in his mind or his soul and because of that he continues to live "In My Father's House". As for me, he finally has decided to accept me as a person instead of just his child and, God forbid, a daughter.